CW00540832

ARSENAL
MINUTE
BY MINUTE

ARSENAL
MINUTE
BY MINUTE

Covering More Than 500 Goals,
Penalties, Red Cards and
Other Intriguing Facts

DAVID JACKSON

First published by Pitch Publishing, 2020

Pitch Publishing
A2 Yeoman Gate
Yeoman Way
Worthing
Sussex
BN13 3QZ
www.pitchpublishing.co.uk
info@pitchpublishing.co.uk

© 2020, David Jackson

Every effort has been made to trace the copyright.
Any oversight will be rectified in future editions at the
earliest opportunity by the publisher.

All rights reserved. No part of this book may be reproduced,
sold or utilised in any form or transmitted in any form or by
any means, electronic or mechanical, including photocopying,
recording or by any information storage and retrieval system,
without prior permission in writing from the Publisher.
A CIP catalogue record is available for this book
from the British Library.

ISBN 978 1 78531 649 4

Typesetting and origination by Pitch Publishing
Printed and bound in India by Replika Press Pvt. Ltd.

Contents

Dedicated to the memory

of José Antonio Reyes

Acknowledgements

Arsenal: Minute by Minute was a hard book to research, but thanks to certain resource outlets, it was made a lot easier. The goal times are taken from various resources, including BBC match reports, Sky Sports games, *Match of the Day*, endless YouTube highlights (and countless newspaper clippings and old match reports that sometimes tested my eyesight to the limit), plus Arsenal FC's official website and various other fan sites and stats platforms such as Opta, Soccerbase, Transfermarkt and 11v11.

Thanks also goes to the dedicated duo that are Andy Kelly and Mark Andrews – the Gunners fans behind the excellent website The Arsenal History (thearsenalhistory. com) which proved an excellent and accurate place to check facts and games – their tireless work and that of many other fan sites proved invaluable for the more hard to research games. Thanks guys and though I learned from them the club is actually called The Arsenal, I've not added 'The' before each mention of the club in the pages that follow.

I'd also like to thank Gunners legend Malcolm Macdonald for very kindly providing the foreword for this book. 'Supermac' only got to enjoy two full seasons at Highbury before a misdiagnosed knee injury ended his career aged 29. His goals per game record was phenomenal and I feel sure he would have broken numerous scoring records for the Gunners had he been able to play two or three more seasons. He was a pleasure to talk to and I thank him for his time and entertaining

ARSENAL: MINUTE BY MINUTE

recollections of his time with the club. Finally, to Paul and Jane Camillin – the tireless siblings who mastermind Pitch Publishing – for green-lighting this series. It's been on Paul's radar for three or four years and finally, we have an end result ...

Introduction

Arsenal FC have an extraordinary history and *Arsenal: Minute by Minute* takes you through the Gunners' matchday history and records the historic goals, incidents, memorable moments and the minute they happened in. From Arsenal's early beginnings and successes to the days of domestic domination; from the great Herbert Chapman era, the Tom Whittaker glory days, Bertie Mee's exciting side of the late 1960s and early 1970s, George Graham's Gunners teams through to Arsène Wenger's Invincibles. Learn about the club's most historic moments or simply relive some truly unforgettable moments from Arsenal's glorious past. You will also discover just how many times a crucial goal has been scored at the same minute so often over the years. From goals scored in the opening few seconds to the last-gasp extra-time winners that have thrilled generations of fans at Highbury, the Emirates or around the world. Included are every goal description from The Invincibles's 49-match unbeaten run – all 112 of them – and countless goals from Thierry Henry, Ian Wright, Alan Sunderland, Liam Brady, Nicolas Anelka and a cast of hundreds from the magnificent players who have graced this club. Legends such as Cliff Bastin and Charlie George are included of course, as well as the odd disappointing moments that Gunners fans will remember well and have played their part in in the club's history.

For a club who once proudly had a terrace named the Clock End, time has always been important to Gunners fans. Now you can see just when those historic, brilliant or occasionally seemingly run-of-the-mill goals were scored, and whether there is any truth in the myth that nobody scores more late goals than Arsenal – particularly during the Arsène Wenger era – and just how many goals resulted in a 1-0 to The Arsenal ...

Enjoy, relive and recall ...

Foreword

By Malcolm Macdonald (1976–79)
Appearances: 108 Goals: 57

In football, matches are defined by minutes and each of the 90 standard minutes played has its own unique life. Whether it's a first-minute goal, a last-minute goal or even one midway through the first half or whatever, every goal matters and that's why *Arsenal: Minute by Minute* was so enjoyable to read.

I'm particularly pleased some of my 57 Arsenal goals are in here, because I remember most of them with great clarity. A player will rarely remember the minute they scored their goals in, unless it is the first or last minute of a half, of course.

My career came to an end while I was at Highbury due to a complicated knee problem that went unnoticed by numerous medical professionals and by the time the problem was discovered, it was too late for me and at 29, I was forced to retire. I scored 29 in my first season and 26 in my second, with my third season effectively ended by injury. It's possible I would have had three or four more years at Highbury had I stayed fit; I might have passed Cliff Bastin's record or I might not have – I'll never know – but for those first two years, I absolutely loved being an Arsenal player.

The last goal I scored for the Gunners was at Stamford Bridge against Chelsea. I remember it well – but I don't remember the minute it was scored in. There was doubt whether I'd ever be fully fit again and though Terry Neill had toyed with playing me in the FA Cup Final against Manchester United the week before, he didn't and he was quite right because Alan Sunderland and Frank Stapleton were magnificent that day.

Chelsea had been relegated, which as a boyhood Fulham fan was fine by me, and the fact I scored in that game as well was particularly special. We had been losing 1-0 and my goal came after the break to earn us a 1-1 draw. It was also my last goal for Arsenal as my loan spell with Djurgårdens in Sweden, which had been meant to build my fitness up over the summer, only accelerated my knee injury and by the time I returned to London, I had grave doubts about my career because I'd already had two knee operations and the specialists were convinced there was nothing wrong with my knee. To cut a long story short, the surgeon who had removed my cartilage at Newcastle had made a mess and because of those errors, the damage to my knee was irreparable. Believe it or not, the specialist who discovered the issues was called Bram Stoker and as this was something of a horror story, it was quite fitting. It took a long time to discover the issue and the third operation which removed the congealed blood that had hardened and caused me so much pain meant I would never play again.

The irony is I was playing the best football of my life and I was scoring goals and playing with some fantastic players, including the best player I'd ever played alongside in Liam Brady. I thoroughly enjoyed playing alongside Frank Stapleton and I'd like to think my hard-edged attitude and the way I pushed him as hard as I could helped make him into a much better player.

But that's all in the past now. Back to scoring goals and one of my favourite games was a 5-3 win over my former club Newcastle United at Highbury. I'd never got on with the Newcastle manager Gordon Lee and for whatever reason, he just didn't like me. He once called me a 'headline grabber' and I said, 'Then how stupid are you? If I'm scoring goals I will be in the headlines, so would you prefer I didn't score anymore?' In the build-up to this game, he had spoken to a newspaper and really dug me out very publicly. He slaughtered me, but I hadn't seen it until Alan Ball brought it to my attention and told all my team-mates to read it. He put it on the noticeboard and on the day of the match, he reminded everyone about the article by saying, 'Listen up, today's the day this guy [me] gets his own back on that bastard!' Due to the freezing conditions, the *Match of the Day* cameras had switched to Highbury because we had undersoil heating. I scored three goals that day and though we were 5-1 up, Newcastle pulled a couple of goals back to make it a bit more respectable, but it was a great day for me and shoved Gordon Lee's words back down his throat.

So back to minutes. The quickest goals I scored in my career were for Newcastle, where I scored one after ten seconds against QPR and an even quicker one in a friendly against St Johnstone, where I scored straight from the kick-off with maybe five seconds or less on the clock.

And if I said 2, 32, 52, 56 and 87, it would mean more to me than most supporters – those were the minutes I scored my five goals in one England game against Cyprus.

So, I'll sign off with an Arsenal goal that I very definitely know the minute it was scored in and that was an injury-time winner away to Manchester United – because it earned me £600! On the journey to Manchester, Liam Brady mentioned that we were 3/1 to win the game. That was big odds in a two-horse race so Liam offered to get a mate of his to put a bet on us to win the game, so Liam, Geordie Armstrong, Alan Ball and myself – each of us putting £200 on.

During the game, we went 1-0 down to a Gordon Hill goal but in the second half, I managed to level the scores. We'd kept the bet between the four of us because even back then, you weren't allowed to bet on matches for obvious reasons, but we'd backed ourselves to win, so I felt there was no real issue. The game went into injury time when the ball came to Frank Stapleton who let fly from about 25 yards and arrowed a shot into the top corner to win the game. The four of us mobbed him and carried him on our shoulders and he had no idea why we were going so mad. So, to me, 90+3 equals £600!

Hope you enjoy the book and I hope your favourite moments have made it in here – just don't ask me which minute they happened in ...

Malcolm Macdonald,
Newcastle, April 2019

Arsenal: Minute by Minute

The clock is ticking ...

10 seconds

28 April 1980

Alan Sunderland gives Arsenal a dream start in the FA Cup semi-final second replay at Villa Park. Having drawn the previous two semi-final encounters against the Merseysiders, the Gunners race out of the blocks with a blistering start to the game. From the kick-off, the ball is played to right-back Pat Rice who launches a long ball towards the edge of the Liverpool box, where it is flicked on into the path of Sunderland who somehow squeezes between two defenders before firing a low shot past Ray Clemence to put Arsenal 1-0 up and send half the stadium delirious in the process.

20 seconds

4 May 2013

Arsenal's quickest Premier League goal to date comes when the Gunners take the lead with only 20 seconds on the clock away to Queens Park Rangers. Armand Traoré's poor header falls to Tomáš Rosický who then finds Mikel Arteta in the box, and the Spanish playmaker slips a clever pass to Theo Walcott who makes no mistake with a clinical finish to score what will prove to be the only goal of the game at Loftus Road.

21 seconds

25 September 2002

The Gunners take the lead in no time at all away to PSV Eindhoven in the Champions League group-stage clash in Holland. In their first attack of the game, Arsenal win possession and the ball is played out to the left for Thierry Henry, who skips past one challenge before looking up and spotting Gilberto Silva's dash into the box. Henry's perfectly timed cross allows the Brazilian to finish from close range with the clock on just 20.7 seconds. Rapid!

29 seconds

23 December 1978

Alan Sunderland gets Arsenal off to an incredible start at White Hart Lane on what will be an unforgettable day for all Gunners fans – and Sunderland in particular. As both teams battle for possession, John Pratt attempts a pass back into his own half to find centre-back John Lacy, but Sunderland is first to the ball and his low shot hits the keeper and flies into the net off the underside of the crossbar.

44 seconds

5 February 2001

Theo Walcott gives Arsenal the lead at St James' Park inside the first minute. In what will prove to be an extraordinary game of two halves, Walcott races on to a pass and clear of the last man before placing a low shot past the Newcastle United keeper from the edge of the box to open the scoring.

2

16 March 2014

Title-chasing Arsenal score with virtually the first attack of the game in the North London derby at White Hart Lane. Tomáš Rosický plays the ball in from the right to Alex Oxlade-Chamberlain who miscontrols the pass but inadvertently returns the ball to Rosický, who instinctively lets fly with a stunning shot from the corner of the box that arrows into the top left of the Spurs net to send the Gunners fans wild – it will be the only goal of the game and is a strike worthy of settling any contest.

28 February 2004

Robert Pires opens the scoring against Charlton with less than 100 seconds played at Highbury. By Arsenal standards of the day, it's a fairly simple goal, with Freddie Ljungberg and Thierry Henry exchanging passes inside the Charlton box before Ljungberg crosses low into the six-yard box and Pires taps home from a yard or so out at the far post – it's his 50th goal for the club.

3

12 October 1996

Ian Wright scores the first goal of the Arsène Wenger era. The Gunners are away to bottom-of-the-table Blackburn Rovers and looking to get the French manager's career in English football off to a winning start, and the game could hardly start any better. Nigel Winterburn plays a long ball into the Rovers box where John Hartson gets up to nod the ball left to Wright, and the prolific striker cuts inside one challenge before planting the ball into the far corner of the net from eight yards.

5 February 2001

Johan Djourou rises to head home an Andrey Arshavin free kick and increase Arsenal's lead (yes, three minutes played and the lead increased!) at St James' Park. To say the Newcastle United fans and players are stunned is something of an understatement, even if the Gunners are challenging for the title, with the game barely begun.

25 April 2004

With the news second-placed Chelsea have lost to Newcastle United earlier in the day, Arsenal travel the short journey across North London to take on Tottenham knowing a point will be enough to win the Premier League with five games to spare. It is an incredible situation for Arsène Wenger's unbeaten side and now they have the chance to seal the title in the backyard of their fiercest rivals. The Gunners take just three minutes to edge ahead with Thierry Henry leading a counter-attack down the left flank before finding Dennis Bergkamp, who crosses low for Patrick Vieira to slide the ball home. Cue mayhem in the White Hart Lane away end.

4

21 December 1991

Anders Limpar sends in a corner that Ian Wright turns home to level the score against Everton at Highbury. The visitors have struck just 60 seconds earlier, but Arsenal hit back immediately with the only notable thing about Wright's goal being that he chests it into the net from close range on what will be a very good afternoon for the Gunners striker – and right-winger.

24 April 1999

Arsenal win an early penalty at the Riverside Stadium after Steve Vickers brings down Nicolas Anelka in the box, leaving the referee with a simple decision to point to the spot. Marc Overmars steps up in Dennis Bergkamp's absence and scuffs his shot – but it still fools the Boro keeper as it rolls past his feet after he's moved slightly to his left to make it 1-0 to the Arsenal.

11 May 2002

Everton gift newly crowned Premier League champions Arsenal an early lead at Highbury. Ashley Cole attacks down the left before sliding a cross into the box. Alan Stubbs blocks the cross but dawdles on the ball, allowing Cole to win back possession and prod the ball across to Dennis Bergkamp who fires home his 14th of the season from close range. It gives the champions a 1-0 lead and maintains a superb record of scoring in every league game this season.

22 February 2003

Arsenal strike early on in what will be a hugely enjoyable last-ever trip to Manchester City's Maine Road. The hosts, who will quit their Moss Side home of 80 years at the end of the campaign, are all at sea with woeful defending playing a huge part in the opening goal, as a gentle pass towards the box from Lauren somehow finds its way through several City defenders and all the way to Dennis Bergkamp, who saunters through for one of the easiest goals he will ever score as he calmly places the ball past Nicky Weaver to put the Premier League leaders and defending champions on their way.

22 November 2003

Arsenal are quickly ahead away to Birmingham City with a goal created from seemingly nothing. Dennis Bergkamp charges down a clearance on the left before cutting inside, midway inside the Birmingham half. He plays a pass across to Thierry Henry who immediately plays it into the path of the overlapping Freddie Ljungberg, who bursts into the box before slotting a low shot past the keeper. Fast, inventive and incisive.

28 February 2004

Arsenal appear to have the points wrapped up with just four minutes on the clock against Charlton Athletic. The visitors must fear they will be on the end of a cricket score as a wonderful team goal makes it 2-0 at Highbury. It starts with Patrick Vieira winning a header in his own half and Dennis Bergkamp receiving the ball. The Dutch playmaker plays it to Robert Pires on the left who then pushes it further down the flank to Vieira who has kept running forward, and his low cross finds Thierry Henry who controls with one foot and fires past the keeper with the other to make it 2-0. Charlton rally somewhat, stem the tide and even pull a goal back in a game that ends 2-1 for the Gunners.

27 May 2017

Arsenal make a superb start to the 2017 FA Cup Final against Chelsea. It is the Gunners' 20th appearance in the final – a record amount for any English club – and Arsène Wenger's side are looking for a 13th success. The opening goal from Alexis Sánchez causes controversy and is initially ruled out for offside, as the Chilean collects the ball on the edge of the penalty area and follows his own attempt to control a clearance into the box before slotting it past Thibaut Courtois from six yards. Replays show Aaron Ramsey hasn't touched the ball at any stage and the offside decision is overruled by the referee, who awards the goal. Chelsea argue Ramsey's presence has distracted Courtois – and they probably have a fair point – but the goal stands.

5

3 May 1998

Needing three points from their remaining three Premier League matches to clinch the title, Arsenal take on Everton at Highbury looking to finish the job on home soil. And the champions elect couldn't start much better with Toffees defender Slaven Bilić heading Emmanuel Petit's deep cross into his own net just five minutes in (despite Tony Adams initially claiming he's had the last touch). It is the perfect start to what will be a perfect day for the Arsenal fans.

24 August 2003

Arsenal get off to a flyer at the Riverside Stadium with a goal inside five minutes. Patrick Vieira picks up possession midway inside the Middlesbrough half before spraying a pass out to his right for Freddie Ljungberg. The Swede hits a low shot that keeper Mark Schwarzer can only parry into the path of Thierry Henry, who taps home from two yards out.

18 October 2003

Arsenal are quickly in front in the London derby against Chelsea. Awarded a free kick on the edge of the Chelsea box, Thierry Henry and Edu stand over the ball – it is Edu who takes it, with his low shot striking the Chelsea wall before deflecting into the bottom corner of Carlo Cudicini's net to give the Gunners a crucial early advantage.

6

16 April 2004

Robert Pires puts Arsenal ahead against Leeds United as the Gunners edge ever closer to the title. And it is another devastating Arsenal goal that dissects the opposition with such ease, as Thierry Henry plays a short pass to Dennis Bergkamp who feeds a lovely ball between two defenders and into the path of Pires, who hits a curling shot into the right of the Leeds net from 18 yards out.

4 October 2015

A delightful goal puts Arsenal 1-0 up against Manchester United at the Emirates. Inevitably, Mesut Özil is at the heart of the move, finding Aaron Ramsey on the edge of the box and then running on to the return pass and sending a low cross in from the right. Alexis Sánchez makes an intelligent run to the near post and his excellent back-heel fools his marker and David de Gea and opens the scoring.

7

12 April 1994

Kevin Campbell gives Arsenal a crucial early lead in the second leg of the European Cup Winners' Cup semi-final. After drawing the first leg in Paris 1-1, the Gunners get off to the perfect start as Lee Dixon probes down the right before delivering a head-high cross into the middle where Campbell quickly adjusts to angle a low header past the keeper, giving the Paris Saint-Germain custodian no chance. It proves to be the only goal of the game and, with a 2-1 aggregate win, the Gunners progress to the European Cup Winners' Cup Final where Parma await.

11 May 2003

Arsenal travel to the Stadium of Light to face Sunderland in the penultimate game of the 2002/03 season. The Gunners, fresh from a 3-2 home loss to Leeds United that ended hopes of back-to-back Premier League titles, are about to embark on a 49-game unbeaten league run starting with this match, and it is fitting that two of the main architects of the team should combine to open the scoring against the Black Cats. A poor ball out of defence is collected by Dennis Bergkamp who plays in Thierry Henry, who finishes with a nonchalant flick from just inside the box that beats the keeper and goes into the top right of the net. A typically polished finish from the French genius and the start of a record-breaking, incredible run by a very special group of players.

1 February 2004

A slip by former Arsenal favourite Nicolas Anelka leads to the opening goal against Manchester City at Highbury. On a rainy night in North London, Anelka loses his footing near the halfway line allowing Arsenal to win possession, and the ball is played to Dennis Bergkamp who plays Thierry Henry in down the left. Henry puts a low cross in towards Freddie Ljungberg but City defender Michaël Tarnat beats him to it and slides the ball past his own keeper from close range.

4 October 2015

The Gunners' blistering start against Manchester United gets even better with a second goal in the space of 74 seconds. The attack starts with Alexis Sánchez flicking the ball into the path of Mesut Özil, who releases Theo Walcott. He bursts into the United box before holding the ball up and spotting Özil in a more central position. He finds the German playmaker with a low ball and Özil calmly places a shot that leaves David de Gea wrong-footed and makes it 2-0 to Arsenal at a rocking Emirates.

8

1 November 2003

A long pass from defence from Ashley Cole finds Thierry Henry who ghosts in behind the Leeds United defence with his electric pace, before placing a low right-foot shot past the Leeds keeper to give the Gunners an early 1-0 lead at Elland Road.

11 May 2005

In what will be the start of the 'Dennis Bergkamp Show', the Gunners take the lead against newly Champions League-qualified Everton. Toffees boss David Moyes has told his side to go out and enjoy the game with the pressure off, but he can't imagine how his side will capitulate. Bergkamp's first assist of what will be a record Premier League victory under Arsène Wenger is a slide-rule pass into the path of Robin van Persie, who fires a low shot home from just inside the box as the rout begins.

7 May 20 06

Needing to better Tottenham's result on the final day of the 2005/06 season to claim the final Champions League berth, Robert Pires puts Arsenal ahead as he prods home from close range against Wigan Athletic. The Gunners have another reason for ensuring they win the game with the fixture the last home game at an emotionally charged Highbury before moving to the new 60,000+ capacity Emirates Stadium.

9

7 May 2003

Arsenal recover from the bitter disappointment of losing out in the Premier League title race with Manchester United by opening the scoring against Southampton after just nine minutes. Robert Pires taps home from close range after Saints keeper Paul Jones saves his first attempt, to lift the somewhat sombre mood of the Gunners fans.

7 February 2004

A lovely Arsenal goal. Brazilian midfielder Edu moves into the Wolverhampton Wanderers half with purpose and plays an incisive ball to Ashley Cole who has made ground down the left, and the England full-back's cross into the box is met with a typically sublime finish from the brilliant Dennis Bergkamp who purposely slices across the ball to send it into the bottom right corner. Nothing is accidental or lucky when Bergkamp is involved, who doesn't seem capable of scoring mere mortal finishes.

9 May 2004

Spaniard José Antonio Reyes hits his second goal in successive games to edge the London derby with Fulham 1-0. It also leaves the Gunners just one game from completing the season unbeaten and confirming their 'Invincibles' tag. The game, played at Fulham's temporary home of Queens Park Rangers's Loftus Road stadium, is settled when Dutch keeper Edwin van der Sar

– outstanding for most of the season for the Cottagers – is caught in possession by Reyes, who has the simplest of tap-ins from close range with what is the only goal of the game for the Premier League champions.

10

1 May 1953

Needing a victory to clinch a record seventh top-flight title, Arsenal fall behind at home to Burnley with just eight minutes played – but the visitors' lead will last just two minutes as Arsenal show the mentality of champions to storm back immediately and level the scores and settle the nerves of the 51,586 Highbury crowd. Tom Forbes's powerful run from the right flank ends with a long-range deflected shot that gives keeper Des Thompson no chance.

5 February 2001

It just keeps getting better for Arsenal who go 3-0 up at St James' Park against Newcastle United. The hosts' suspect defending is again exploited with Theo Walcott's run and cross from the right of the box finding Robin van Persie, who strokes home from six yards to seemingly seal three points for Arsène Wenger's side. Seemingly ...

2 December 2018

Arsenal take an early lead in the North London derby at the Emirates. As the ball is crossed into the box, Jan Vertonghen raises an arm and makes clear contact resulting in a penalty kick. Despite the protestations of the Belgian defender, Pierre-Emerick Aubameyang coolly slots home from the spot to put the Gunners 1-0 up.

11

1 May 1980

Arsenal finally see off Liverpool in (incredibly) a third FA Cup semi-final replay. Two evenly matched sides have drawn all three of the previous semi-final matches in the days before penalty shoot-outs and many wonder whether they can ever be separated. Hillsborough, Villa Park (twice) and Coventry City's Highfield Road have all hosted the matches that have ended up 0-0, 1-1 and 1-1, as both sides have attempted to book a place at Wembley. Inevitably, it is an individual error that eventually settles the contest and there is no shortage of irony that it is a former Gunners player who makes the mistake that leads to the winning goal. Pat Rice plays Frank Stapleton in on the right of the box but Ray Kennedy seems to have it covered for Liverpool. Former Arsenal favourite Kennedy, however, loses his balance as he's about to clear his lines and Stapleton crosses the loose ball into the box, where Brian Talbot arrives to head down and past Ray Clemence for what will be the only goal of the game. Bizarrely, this is the fifth meeting between the teams in just 19 days, with four FA Cup clashes and a First Division clash at Anfield and the sixth meeting that campaign, with three games ending 1-1, two ending 0-0 and this one ending 1-0 (to the Arsenal!). Both sides, it's fair to say, must be heartily sick of each other!

4 April 1993

Arsenal and Spurs battle out a North London derby at Wembley in the semi-final of the FA Cup – and it is the

Gunners who score the only goal of what turns out to be a largely disappointing game early on. Ray Parlour's burst towards the Spurs box is ended with a foul and wins a free kick in a terrific position. Paul Merson weighs up his options before he whips in a free kick towards the far post where captain Tony Adams arrives on the blind side of Tottenham keeper Eric Thorstvedt to head the ball home and send the Arsenal fans wild.

2 March 2002

An individual goal that is described as one of the best Arsenal have ever scored sets the Gunners on their way to a crucial three points at St James' Park. The move begins with Patrick Vieira winning the ball in his own half before the ball works its way to Robert Pires who plays it to the feet of Dennis Bergkamp, whose touch 'around the corner' is utterly sublime and as the Dutch master completes his pirouette around his mesmerised marker, he finds himself with just Shay Given to beat, which he does with consummate ease to make it 1-0 versus Newcastle United. Breathtakingly brilliant from a supremely gifted footballer.

14 December 2003

An early Dennis Bergkamp goal proves to be enough to earn all three points for the Gunners at Highbury. For once, it is not Thierry Henry, Robert Pires or Freddie Ljungberg who provides the assist – it is the unlikely figure of central defender Kolo Touré, who picks up the ball on the right, takes on and beats the full-back with ease before moving towards goal, cutting the ball back into the six-yard box where Bergkamp makes the finish from close range look simple.

24 September 2016

Arsenal are gifted an early lead in the Premier League home clash against Chelsea. Gary Cahill's attempt at a back pass from just inside his own half is intercepted by Alexis Sánchez who races clear, and as a desperate Cahill and the keeper converge, the Chilean dinks a delightful chip between both to put the Gunners 1-0 up at the Emirates.

12

12 May 1979

Arsenal draw first blood in the 1979 FA Cup Final against Manchester United. Frank Stapleton picks up the ball on the right flank and spots David Price's clever run into the United box with a low ball to feet. Price skips past one challenge before cutting the ball back into the six-yard box where Alan Sunderland and Brian Talbot arrive almost simultaneously to scramble home the opening goal from close range. TV replays later credit Talbot with the final touch but the goal is largely forgotten in the late drama that is yet to come ...

2 May 1981

In a game of huge significance for both Arsenal and Aston Villa, it is the Gunners who deservedly take an early lead. Arsenal are looking for a win that will secure a UEFA Cup spot, while visitors Villa need one point to secure the Division One title. Highbury is packed to the rafters with perhaps 10,000 travelling fans from the Midlands crammed into the Clock End hoping to see their team crowned champions. The opening goal comes when Kenny Sansom's free kick on the left of the Villa box finds Alan Sunderland who gets too much on his header, and then Brian McDermott manages to keep the ball in play by nodding towards the penalty spot where Willie Young volleys a low shot into the bottom-right corner.

22 February 2003

Arsenal double their lead against Manchester City with yet more terrible defending from the Blues at Maine Road. If the first goal contains more than an element of self-destruction, the second is even worse as Richard Dunne lazily tries to clear the ball from just outside his own box, but only finds the lurking Thierry Henry. The Gunners striker then almost cruelly waltzes around Dunne towards the byline before playing a low ball in for Robert Pires to sweep home from close range and make it 2-0 with only 12 minutes played.

11 May 2005

A goal created by the vision and brilliance of Dennis Bergkamp, who sends a 40-yard pass to Robin van Persie on the left flank – he gets to the byline before crossing back to the edge of the box where Robert Pires fires a low shot goalwards. Everton keeper Richard Wright makes a fine save, but the ball is pushed upwards and out to Pires, following his own shot, who sends a header looping over the keeper and in off the underside of the crossbar to make it 2-0.

13

31 March 1971

In a classic midweek evening FA Cup semi-final replay against Stoke City – the sort that only seems to happen in the 1970s – Arsenal take an early lead. There is nothing complicated about the goal which is simplicity in itself, as a George Armstrong corner is floated in towards the penalty spot where George Graham climbs higher than anyone else to power a header just underneath the crossbar and out of reach of the keeper and defenders on the line and sends half of Villa Park wild.

7 February 1978

Malcolm Macdonald puts Arsenal ahead at Anfield with a cool finish from close range at the Kop end. There seems little danger for Liverpool as the Gunners win a throw-in on the left. Sammy Nelson's long throw clears Tommy Smith and Frank Stapleton picks up the ball and plays a short pass beyond Emlyn Hughes to leave Supermac with just Ray Clemence to beat – which he does with ease – to give his side a crucial 1-0 lead in the League Cup semi-final first leg.

21 December 1991

Arsenal go 2-1 up at Highbury against Everton and it is the same combination that results in the first goal who strike again. A long ball out to the right sees Anders Limpar race down the flank and into the box and the Swedish international plays a perfect low ball across the six-yard box, and Ian Wright meets it by sliding home a left-foot shot for his second of the game from four yards out.

5 April 1998

Christopher Wreh becomes the first Liberian to score in an FA Cup semi-final when he gives Arsenal the lead against Wolverhampton Wanderers at Villa Park. A poor kick out from the Wolves keeper is collected by Patrick Vieira who drives towards goal before laying the ball off to his right where Wreh drills a low shot into the bottom corner. It will prove to be the only goal of the game and as a result deny Wolves a first FA Cup Final for 38 years.

9 December 2000

Gilles Grimandi plays a 60-yard pass to the feet of Thierry Henry who takes a superb first touch to nudge through the legs of his marker in the process on the corner of the Newcastle United box, before drilling an angled low shot past Shay Given from 15 yards to put the Gunners 1-0 up. Simple, but brilliant from Henry.

16 November 2002

One of the great North London derby goals as Thierry Henry, deep inside his own half, shrugs off the challenge of Matthew Etherington before moving at speed up the pitch. As he reaches the Spurs box, he shifts inside past one challenge and then another before curling a low left-foot shot past the keeper from 18 yards to put the Gunners 1-0 up against Spurs at Highbury. A fantastic solo goal and the sort only Henry seems capable of scoring.

24 August 2003

The Gunners quickly double their lead away to Middlesbrough with a classy goal from Gilberto Silva. The move that leads to the goal begins down the left flank with Ashley Cole and Robert Pires combining well before Pires checks inside to see his options in the box, chips over the perfect cross towards the advancing Gilberto and the Brazilian meets it on the volley to power a low shot past the keeper.

26 December 2003

Arsenal – who have drawn three of their previous four Premier League matches, dropping points against Bolton Wanderers, Leicester City and Fulham – return to form against Wolves on Boxing Day 2003 to maintain their unbeaten start to the season. The opening goal is a scrappy affair, with a Thierry Henry corner causing a scramble with Patrick Vieira managing to get a touch, but it is Wolves's Jody Craddock who gets the decisive touch and credit for the goal. Nobody is complaining.

24 January 2018

A game of head pinball in the Chelsea box ends with the ball in the back of the net. Trailing 1-0 in the second leg of the Carabao Cup semi-final at the Emirates, Nacho Monreal heads a corner towards goal – it hits Marcos Alonso and then immediately rebounds off Antonio Rüdiger to beat Willy Caballero and level the scores. A bizarre own goal but a welcome leveller on the night.

14

20 September 1998

Arsenal get off to a fine start against Manchester United at Highbury. When a free kick is awarded on the right of the United penalty area, Stephen Hughes whips in a dangerous cross and Tony Adams times his leap perfectly to glance a header past Peter Schmeichel and into the far corner of the net to put the Gunners 1-0 up.

25 September 2004

Ashley Cole scores a goal that any one of the galaxy of gifted Gunners forwards would be proud of to beat Manchester City at the City of Manchester Stadium. Thierry Henry probes down the left flank before passing to José Antonio Reyes – his attempted pass back to Henry is half intercepted by City's Richard Dunne, but Cole quickly nips it off his toes and running across the box he nonchalantly flicks the ball into the bottom-left corner with the outside of his left boot. A quality goal that proves also to be the winner as the Gunners stretch their magnificent run to 47 Premier League games without loss.

13 January 2016

Arsenal take just four minutes to level the scores at Anfield. Trailing to Roberto Firmino's tenth-minute opener, the Gunners – who go into the game two points clear of Leicester City in the title race – silence the Kop as Joel Campbell slips a pass into Aaron Ramsey in the

Liverpool box and the Welsh midfielder drills a low shot into the bottom-right corner to make it 1-1.

24 September 2016

Arsenal make it two goals in the space of three minutes to open up a 2-0 lead over Chelsea in the London derby at the Emirates. Alex Iwobi finds Héctor Bellerín's dart into the box and the Spanish full-back plays a pass immediately into the six-yard box, where Theo Walcott makes no mistake to double the Gunners' lead.

15

1 May 1953

Arsenal recover from going behind early on to lead Burnley 2-1 with only 15 minutes on the clock. After winning a corner when Don Roper's shot is saved by Thompson, Roper's corner finds Jimmy Logie who dummies the ball and Doug Lishman drills home a low volley to put the Gunners on course for the title with his 22nd league goal of the season.

31 March 1979

Republic of Ireland striker Frank Stapleton breaks the deadlock in the FA Cup semi-final against Wolves at Villa Park. David Price receives the ball midway inside the Wolves half, prods it past one challenge before laying a short pass to Stapleton, who drops a shoulder and creates a yard of space for himself before arrowing a low right-foot shot into the bottom-left corner of the net from 20 yards out.

6 January 2003

FA Cup holders Arsenal ease past third-tier Oxford United in the third round at Highbury. The opening goal is typical of Dennis Bergkamp – measured and precise – as the Dutchman collects the ball on the edge of the box before sizing up the situation and placing the ball out of the keeper's reach with his usual calmness. It is his 100th goal for the Gunners and at 33, a timely reminder of his class and continued influence on the team. Arsenal go on to win the game 2-0.

22 February 2003

Arsenal race into a 3-0 lead at Maine Road as Manchester City's defending goes from bad to worse. Martin Keown plays a superb 60-yard ball out of defence into the path of Thierry Henry, who controls the pass and then fires a left-foot shot almost instantly to leave keeper Nicky Weaver so flat-footed he can only watch as the ball finds its way just inside the right-hand post. Three goals to the good and just 15 minutes played, the City fans must be fearing a cricket score by the rampant Gunners and many head down the tunnel for an early pint to drown their sorrows!

21 February 2004

Reeling from conceding a goal against Chelsea after just 27 seconds, the Gunners show their mettle at Stamford Bridge by quickly drawing level with 15 minutes played. As so often, it's an individual piece of brilliance that creates the opportunity from Dennis Bergkamp, who spots Patrick Vieira on the edge of the box in space and curls a pass into the Frenchman's path from midway inside the Chelsea half, and Vieira spins and follows the ball into the box before sliding home a low shot to make it 1-1.

21 September 2010

Henri Lansbury slides home the opening goal of the Carling Cup third-round clash with Spurs at White Hart Lane. Making only his sixth appearance for Arsenal, Lansbury is on the end of a Jack Wilshere cross to score what will be the only goal of his career with the Gunners.

22 March 2014

What should be a day of celebration turns into a disaster for Arsenal who see their Premier League title hopes effectively ended at Stamford Bridge. In Arsène Wenger's 1,000th game in charge of the Gunners, league leaders Chelsea quickly go 2-0 up, but on 15 minutes, referee Andre Marriner makes a huge error as Alex Oxlade-Chamberlain tips Eden Hazard's shot around the post. The official correctly points to the spot, but then shows a straight red card to Kieran Gibbs who, despite Oxlade-Chamberlain and other players trying to explain Gibbs's innocence, is forced to leave the pitch. Arsenal go on to lose 6-0 to Jose Mourinho's side – and it is the Portuguese manager who beats Wenger in his 500th game in charge as well. A day to forget for everyone in red and white.

8 March 2018

Arsenal get the early away goal they need in the Europa League round of 16 first leg against AC Milan. The Gunners, who ten years earlier had become the first English side to beat Milan on home soil at the same stage of the Champions League, take the lead when Henrikh Mkhitaryan bags his first goal for the club, cutting in from the left to fire in with the aid of a deflection off Milan skipper Leonardo Bonucci.

16

26 April 1930

Alex James's quick reaction to Cliff Bastin's free kick puts Arsenal 1-0 up in the 1930 FA Cup Final against a Huddersfield Town side who dominate the era. But this represents a changing of the guard in English football. It is the Gunners' first appearance in the cup final and Wembley goes wild as James's snap shot from the edge of the box puts Herbert Chapman's side a goal to the good. Chapman has famously won three top-flight titles with Huddersfield Town before becoming Arsenal manager and the feeling is that if anyone can mastermind the Terriers' downfall, it is Chapman.

8 April 1978

Taking on Second Division Orient, who are making their first-ever FA Cup semi-final appearance, Malcolm Macdonald puts the Gunners ahead at Stamford Bridge. It's just the sort of start Orient (in their pre-Leyton days) have feared and it sets the tone for the rest of the game, with the second-tier side never quite able to threaten a giant-killing over their North London neighbours. The goal, incidentally, would be credited as an own goal by today's rulings, with Macdonald's wayward volley striking Orient left-back Bill Roffey who can do little to get out of the way and the ball ends up in the back of the net. Of course, Supermac claimed it and the authorities credited it accordingly! He later says it is the correct decision as nobody could prove he hasn't meant what has happened!

9 December 2000

The Gunners score a second goal against Newcastle United in three minutes to make it 2-0 at Highbury. Nwankwo Kanu lifts an excellent pass past a couple of defenders and into the path of Ray Parlour and the 'Romford Pelé' strikes a superb shot with the outside of his right boot that arrows past Shay Given and in off the far post from the right of the box.

1 November 2003

A counter-attack down the right leads to Arsenal doubling their lead at Elland Road. Freddie Ljungberg cuts inside from the wing before playing a low pass into the path of Gilberto Silva who misses the ball, but it continues into the path of Robert Pires who finishes neatly with an angled shot and gives his side a 2-0 lead over Leeds United.

20 March 2004

Arsenal continue their season of spectacular goals with another superb strike from the excellent Robert Pires. There seems little danger for a well-marshalled Bolton Wanderers defence when Edu plays a pass from the right to Dennis Bergkamp on the edge of the box, but as soon as the ball lands at his feet he flicks it into the path of Pires who has one touch and then fires a shot into the top-right corner of the Bolton net from 18 yards to put the Gunners 1-0 up at Highbury. Devastating.

14 February 2016

A rare entry in our minute by minute guide – a superb save – but one well worth recalling. Hosting surprise Premier League leaders Leicester City, the Gunners need three points to close the gap to just two at the top, but the Foxes should go ahead when Marc Albrighton sends in a superb cross that finds Jamie Vardy, who does everything right as he nods down firmly to the left of Petr Cech from six yards out – it looks a certain goal but Cech somehow gets down to not only stop the ball on the line but hold on to it as Vardy moves in. A quite breathtaking save and given what happens later in the game, arguably a match-winning save, too.

17

5 May 1999

The game Arsenal fans have been dreading might derail their hopes of winning the title finally arrives with just three matches of the season remaining. Locked in a fascinating battle with Manchester United, there is a real possibility the eventual champions could win the league on goal difference – but only if both sides win their remaining matches. Spurs fans are desperate to see their side beat Arsenal and be the team to end those title aspirations, but it is the Gunners who strike first with the brilliance of Dennis Bergkamp at the heart of the move. Nicolas Anelka collects the ball just inside the Spurs half and plays a short pass to Bergkamp behind him – the Dutchman looks up and then plays a defence-splitting through ball into the path of Emmanuel Petit who takes a first touch that slightly lifts the ball off the ground before gently lobbing the onrushing keeper from the edge of the box to put Arsenal 1-0 up. A brilliant finish from the French midfielder and his first league goal of the year.

7 May 2003

The Gunners double their lead against Southampton after Nwankwo Kanu and Thierry Henry combine well before Giovanni van Bronckhorst sets up Jermaine Pennant, making his Premier League debut for Arsenal, to finish calmly and make it 2-0 at Highbury.

4 October 2009

Thomas Vermaelen puts Arsenal level against Blackburn Rovers as he rounds off a slick passing move with a crisp, low, left-foot shot from the edge of the box that gives keeper Paul Robinson no chance on what will be the start of a long afternoon for the Rovers no. 1 ...

17 May 2014

Arsenal, appearing in a record-equalling 18th FA Cup Final, are still reeling from the shock of conceding two goals in the opening ten minutes against unfancied Hull City who are making their first ever appearance in the final. The rampant Tigers have also seen another effort cleared off the line as the Humberside outfit look to get the game wrapped up as quickly as possible. Needing to find a way back into the game before it runs away from them, a free kick is awarded some 25 yards out for the Gunners. It needs something special to bring Arsène Wenger's side back into the game and Spain international Santi Cazorla provides it, thumping a superb shot into the top right-hand corner of the net to halve the deficit. Suddenly, the game has a different complexion to it.

18

20 April 1950

Arsenal go into the 1950 FA Cup Final looking to win the trophy for the first time in 14 years. Captain Joe Mercer leads the team out against Liverpool in front of a 100,000-strong Wembley crowd. And the Gunners fans don't have to wait too long for the opening goal, with a set piece undoing the Merseysiders as Denis Compton's corner is turned in at close range by Reg Lewis. Compton is also a first-class cricketer who will make 78 appearances for England, scoring close to 6,000 runs. One for the trivia questions in the pub!

26 September 2003

Arsenal break the deadlock as torrential rain drenches the Highbury crowd. And the weather plays a part in the opening goal as Lauren's cross from the right flank is miscued by Newcastle United skipper Titus Bramble, whose attempted clearance falls to the one man the Magpies would have least wanted it to – Thierry Henry – and the Arsenal striker duly finishes at the far post.

17 May 2006

Jens Lehmann gets an unwanted first as he is shown a straight red card for bringing down Samuel Eto'o outside the box in the 2006 Champions League Final against Barcelona. Lehmann is the first player to be sent off in a Champions League Final and is replaced by Manuel

Almunia, following the withdrawal of Robert Pires. The Gunners make a real fist of the game, but despite leading until the 76th minute, the Catalan side score two late goals to win 2-1. What the score might have been with 11 versus 11 will never be known.

18 April 2009

Arsenal take the lead in an all-London FA Cup semi-final at Wembley. Emmanuel Adebayor starts the move that leads to the opening goal of the game as he plays in Kieran Gibbs, who bursts forward from the back and then sends in a cross that Theo Walcott hits towards goal before clipping Ashley Cole en route and leaving Petr Cech stranded.

26 September 2015

Trailing 1-0 to Leicester City – who have also hit the woodwork twice in a frantic start to the game at the King Power Stadium – Arsenal draw level with a counter-attack goal that the Foxes themselves would be proud of. The ball is cleared out to the left and to Santi Cazorla inside the Leicester half – the Spaniard threads a pass into Theo Walcott's path and, pursued by two defenders, he outpaces both, running into the box before sending a low drive past Kasper Schmeichel and inside the right post.

19

22 February 2003

Sol Campbell powers home a fourth goal as a scintillating Arsenal continue to take Kevin Keegan's Manchester City to the cleaners. The first three goals have been largely the result of some awful defending by the hosts, but the fourth is fairly straightforward by comparison as the irrepressible Thierry Henry – who has scored the third and made the second – floats a corner into the six-yard box for Campbell to rise highest and thump a header past Nicky Weaver to send most of the fans at Maine Road out of their seats – and a fair few probably on their way back to their cars.

16 October 2004

Arsenal recover from going behind after just three minutes at home to Aston Villa. Thierry Henry is the creator, skipping past a couple of challenges on the left flank before being felled in the box by a late challenge. Robert Pires coolly converts the spot kick to make it 1-1.

4 October 2015

Wow! A killer third goal for the Gunners with less than 20 minutes on the clock courtesy of a thunderous shot from Alexis Sánchez. The Chilean receives the ball from Theo Walcott on the left of the Manchester United box and rides his luck as he moves past his first challenge and then, thanks to some slack United defending, decides to let fly from 20 yards – and how – with a right-foot howitzer into the top-right corner to make it 3-0 and, though nobody knew it at that point, complete the scoring for the afternoon.

30 October 2019

Lucas Torreira scores the first Arsenal goal of a remarkable game away to Liverpool. Trailing 1-0 in the Carabao Cup tie at Anfield to an early Mustafi own goal, the Gunners level when Torreira is first to the ball as Liverpool reserve keeper Caoimhín Kelleher pushes a shot out from Bukayo Saka – but only as far as the Uruguayan, who slots home from close range to make it 1-1.

20

6 September 1913

An historic goal – if not one for Arsenal – as Leicester Fosse's Tommy Benfield becomes the first player to score a competitive goal in the Gunners' brand new Highbury stadium. The ground, not fully completed but now able to host matches, is attended by 20,000 fans and though an early blow, Arsenal recover to win 2-1.

8 April 1978

Orient realise their fairy-tale hopes are probably going to crash and burn when a second wicked deflection of the game puts Arsenal 2-0 up in the FA Cup semi-final at Stamford Bridge. Malcolm Macdonald has seen his first goal strike a defender and go into the net and his second of the afternoon also has more than a hint of good fortune. As a cross comes into the six-yard box, the ball is only half cleared to Macdonald eight yards out – he chests the ball down before volleying towards goal where former Gunners schoolboy Glenn Roeder attempts to head it clear but only wrong-foots his own keeper to double Arsenal's advantage. It is Supermac's day and definitely not Orient's!

18 April 1993

Arsenal recover quickly after going behind to an early goal against Sheffield Wednesday in the 1993 League Cup Final at Wembley. American midfielder John Harkes has put the Owls ahead on eight minutes, but the Gunners, looking for only a second-ever League Cup triumph, equalise with a superb half-volley from the edge of the box courtesy of the gifted Paul Merson who sees his right-foot shot curl away from the Wednesday keeper into the top right of the net to make it 1-1.

15 May 1993

In what proves to be an epic series of battles with Sheffield Wednesday during the 1992/93 season, Arsenal take the lead in the 1993 FA Cup Final against the Owls. Though Wednesday start the game much better, it is the Gunners who open the scoring when a free kick into the area is nodded across the six-yard box by Andy Linighan for Ian Wright to power a header home. The South Yorkshire side will level after the break and force a replay at Wembley a week later.

4 May 1994

Arsenal take on Parma in the European Cup Winners' Cup Final at the Parken Stadium in Copenhagen. In a close game, Alan Smith pounces on a defensive error as Lorenzo Minotti mishits an attempted overhead kick clearance and the Gunners striker is on hand to send a superb half-volley past the Parma goalkeeper Luca Bucci and into the net from just inside the box. It proves to be the only goal of the game and gives the Gunners their biggest European success yet, and the celebrations last long into the night in Denmark in what is a landmark moment for the club.

13 September 1997

A momentous occasion for all who witness it as Ian Wright equals Cliff Bastin's record of 178 goals for Arsenal when he levels the score at home to Bolton Wanderers. Wright has been stuck on 177 goals for four weeks and three matches but he finally gets his record-equalling goal as he latches on to Dennis Bergkamp's pass to fire home from close range. In all the excitement, he lifts his shirt to reveal a T-shirt message '179 – just done it!' Even though he hadn't! Not yet, anyway ...

7 May 2003

A rampant Arsenal go 3-0 up with just 20 minutes played when Jermaine Pennant heads home from close range after Southampton keeper Paul Jones parries Thierry Henry's deflected shot in the penultimate game of the 2002/03 season. If the Saints – who have more than an element of 'already on the beach' about their start to the game – fear the worst, they are right to do so ...

26 December 2003

Arsenal go 2-0 up against Wolves and it is all thanks to the combative nature of a Patrick Vieira at the very top of his game. The French powerhouse wins possession from Jody Craddock (who has earlier scored an own goal) 30 yards out and then drives into the box before stopping, looking to his right and playing a simple pass to Thierry Henry who slides the ball home from six yards out. Craddock, meanwhile, waits for the ground to open up and swallow him.

14 January 2006

Arsenal take the lead against Middlesbrough on what will be the start of a very long afternoon for the visitors. The Gunners have gone close once or twice before finally breaking through with a stunning Thierry Henry strike. Freddie Ljungberg then gets in behind the Boro defence before sending a slightly deflected cross towards the edge of the box, where Henry fires a powerful volley home from 18 yards with the Boro keeper barely moving.

24 October 2010

Arsenal take full advantage of Manchester City having a player sent off early on to take command of the Premier League clash at the Etihad Stadium. Samir Nasri exchanges passes with Andrey Arshavin before firing a shot past Joe Hart to give the Gunners a 1-0 lead against emerging title rivals City. It is Nasri's seventh goal in seven games, with the former Marseille playmaker becoming ever more integral to Arsène Wenger's side.

29 December 2012

Considering there will be ten goals in the Premier League clash with Newcastle United, it is amazing the first 20 minutes at the Emirates has remained goalless. That all ends and the fun begins when Lukas Podolski plays a ball down the left for Theo Walcott, whose pace takes him clear into the box before he places a measured low shot across the keeper and into the far corner to make it 1-0.

1 November 2016

Granit Xhaka pulls a quick goal back after Arsenal have fallen 2-0 behind to Ludogorets in the Champions League group stage clash in Bulgaria. The Gunners are expected to stroll home against a side they have beaten 6-0 at the Emirates in the first meeting, but the hosts score twice in the opening 15 minutes before Xhaka halves the deficit with a low shot from 15 yards after good work by Mesut Özil.

21

1 May 1953

Arsenal go 3-1 up with just 21 minutes on the clock in a game they must win to secure a seventh top-division title. Don Roper and Ben Marden combine to send Jimmy Logie free and he nudges the ball past Des Thompson from close range to give the Gunners breathing space. Despite the frantic start, it will be Arsenal's last goal of the game, with Burnley reducing the arrears on 75 minutes and the hosts having to hold on to win 3-2. The result sees Arsenal finish level on points with Preston North End, so goal average has to settle the outcome. Goal average is worked out by dividing the number of goals scored by the number of goals conceded, meaning the Gunners win the title by just 0.099 on goal average in one of the closest top-flight finishes imaginable.

5 December 2001

Freddie Ljungberg gives Arsenal a vital early lead in the Champions League group stage clash with Juventus. Needing nothing less than a win to keep hopes of progression to the knockout stages alive, the Gunners withstand early pressure and make the vital breakthrough first as Lauren drifts inside two challenges on the right before his low cross is deflected to Patrick Vieira on the edge of the box – he shifts it to the right before firing in a shot that Gianluigi Buffon uncharacteristically spills, and Ljungberg is first to the loose ball, forcing it past Buffon's attempt at redemption and into the back of the net.

21 February 2004

The Gunners complete their recovery against Chelsea with a second – and match-winning – goal at Stamford Bridge. Despite having gone behind inside a minute, Arsenal demonstrate their title credentials by levelling and then going ahead when Thierry Henry's inswinging corner is missed by keeper Neil Sullivan, the ball hits Eidur Gudjohnsen and falls to Edu, who scrambles a low shot into the unguarded net to make it 2-1 and with no further scoring, secure three vital points.

18 October 2005

Thierry Henry comes on to replace the injured José Antonio Reyes after 15 minutes of Arsenal's Champions League tie away to Sparta Prague. The French striker is on 184 goals for the Gunners and is just one away from equalling Ian Wright's all-time goals record, which has stood for eight years and 35 days. Henry, who has spent the previous six weeks out with a groin strain, takes just six minutes to move level with Wright with a typically stunning effort from the edge of the box. After collecting a long ball from Kolo Touré, Henry curls a shot with the outside of his boot to give the Czech keeper no chance and put the Gunners 1-0 up.

10 August 2014

Santi Cazorla puts Arsenal ahead in the 2014 FA Community Shield against defending Premier League champions Manchester City. In glorious Wembley sunshine, the ball falls to the Spaniard on the edge of the City box and he quickly shifts on to his left foot before drilling a low shot into the bottom-right corner from 18 yards out.

15 September 2019

Sead Kolašinac picks up the ball on the halfway line before driving towards the Watford box – he then plays a pass inside to Pierre-Emerick Aubameyang who spins and drills home a low shot past Ben Foster from just inside the penalty area to give the Gunners the lead at Vicarage Road.

22

5 April 1997

Arsenal take the lead against Chelsea with a goal from Ian Wright. Both sides have early chances but it is the Gunners who break the deadlock at Stamford Bridge, as Dennis Bergkamp plays a superb pass into the path of Wright who drills a low, angled shot past Frode Grodås to put Arsenal 1-0 up.

24 August 2003

The Gunners' blistering start at the Riverside Stadium continues with Middlesbrough left chasing shadows as Arsenal cut their defence to shreds time after time. The third goal of the afternoon comes when Robert Pires releases Thierry Henry down the left and the France striker moves towards the box, patiently waiting for the right moment to flick a cross into the six-yard area, where Sylvain Wiltord expertly guides a volley to the right of Mark Schwarzer to make it 3-0. Sublime play from Arsène Wenger's irresistible team.

28 August 2004

Arsenal take the lead away to Norwich City and the goal is largely down to the electric pace of Thierry Henry, who speeds past a couple of challenges as he heads for the byline and his low cross into the middle evades a couple of defenders and arrives perfectly for José Antonio Reyes, who makes no mistake from close range.

14 January 2006

Philippe Senderos scores Arsenal's second goal in as many minutes to put his team 2-0 up at Highbury against Middlesbrough. José Antonio Reyes whips in a deep corner from the right and Senderos rises higher than anyone else to power a header past Brad Jones and put the Gunners firmly in the driving seat.

23

16 May 1998

It is to be a case of third time lucky in the 1998 FA Cup Final against Newcastle United. The Gunners have met the Magpies twice before in the final – and lost on each occasion – but this time will be different as Arsenal look to complete the coveted league and FA Cup double. Midway through the first half, the Gunners take the lead. Emmanuel Petit's clever lofted pass into the path of Marc Overmars still leaves the Dutchman plenty of work, but after shrugging off the challenge of Alessandro Pistone, he then toe-pokes the ball past keeper Shay Given to make it 1-0.

7 May 2003

Arsenal continue to run riot at Highbury with a fourth goal against a punch-drunk Southampton. With barely half of the first period played, the Gunners wrap up the points when Thierry Henry puts Robert Pires clear and the French forward drills a low shot past Saints keeper Paul Jones, who is beaten on his near post.

15 August 2004

Arsenal begin the defence of the Premier League title they've won the previous season with a stylish performance at Goodison Park. The Gunners threaten the Everton defence several times before Dennis Bergkamp marks his 500th league appearance of his career (including Ajax and

Inter Milan) perfectly with the opening goal. José Antonio Reyes is challenged as he bursts into the box, but the ball only falls to Thierry Henry who passes to Bergkamp to finish with his usual panache and mark his personal milestone in style.

17 November 2012

The North London derby takes another twist in Arsenal's favour. Having gone behind to Emmanuel Adebayor's early goal, the former Gunners striker is then red carded on 18 minutes. Things get worse for Tottenham five minutes after that as terrific work by Theo Walcott sees the winger manage to get in a cross from the right, and Per Mertesacker powers a header home from eight yards to make it 1-1.

24

20 March 2004

The Gunners double their lead at home to Bolton Wanderers. The move starts with Edu winning possession and playing a short pass to Robert Pires on the halfway line – he threads a ball into the path of Thierry Henry down the left channel and he whips in a cross towards the unmarked Dennis Bergkamp – it looks to have a tad too much weight on it as it moves across Bergkamp but he manages to stretch and still get a low shot in that beats the keeper on his near post to make it 2-0.

2 August 2015

Alex Oxlade-Chamberlain scores a stunning goal to win the FA Community Shield showdown with Chelsea. At a sun-drenched Wembley (isn't it always?), the Gunners lay down a marker for the season ahead as Theo Walcott finds Oxlade-Chamberlain on the right of the Chelsea box – he cuts inside one challenge and then curls a powerful shot into the top left-hand corner from 12 yards with his weaker left foot. It proves to be the only goal of the game and gives Arsène Wenger his first win over a José Mourinho side in some 14 attempts.

25

28 April 1970

Trailing 3-1 from the first leg of the Inter-Cities Fairs Cup Final against Anderlecht, Eddie Kelly sends a packed Highbury wild with a sumptuous 20-yard strike. The ball comes to Kelly on the edge of the box and after cutting inside one challenge he sends a fierce right-foot shot past the unsighted Belgian keeper who barely moves as the ball flies past him. It makes the aggregate 2-3 in Anderlecht's favour, but the momentum is now very much with the Gunners.

13 September 1997

Five minutes after revealing a T-shirt proclaiming he has beaten Cliff Bastin's record of 178 goals, Ian Wright scores the goal that actually sets the new scoring record for the Gunners. Dennis Bergkamp's run into the box and shot falls to Patrick Vieira, who slides the ball into Wright's path for the simplest of chances to put Arsenal 2-1 up against Bolton Wanderers. An historic moment for a wonderful striker who this time displays his T-shirt correctly!

25 November 2003

Thierry Henry gives Arsenal the lead at the San Siro in a Champions League group stage clash with Inter Milan. A lovely, slick passing move involving Robert Pires and Ashley Cole sees the ball played back to Henry on the edge of the box and his powerful side-footed shot from the edge of the area finds the bottom-right corner to put the Gunners 1-0 up.

20 March 2003

Arsenal take the lead at Stamford Bridge in the FA Cup quarter-final tie against Chelsea. The Gunners draw first blood when Sylvain Wiltord drives towards the Chelsea penalty area before playing the ball out wide to Patrick Vieira who puts in a dangerous low cross into the six-yard box, and Chelsea skipper John Terry's attempted clearance instead beats his own goalkeeper to give the visitors a 1-0 lead.

22 August 2004

Thierry Henry opens his account for the 2004/05 season to put Arsenal 1-0 up at Highbury against Middlesbrough. In what will be a pulsating game, José Antonio Reyes, becoming ever more influential for the Gunners, plays a superb long ball from his own half and Henry allows the ball to bounce once before calmly lobbing it over Mark Schwarzer – though the visitors are far from out of this contest and stun Highbury by scoring the next three goals of the game to put the Gunners' 41-match unbeaten league run under serious threat ...

9 March 2015

A superb team goal gives Arsenal the lead at Old Trafford in the FA Cup sixth-round tie with Manchester United. The Gunners threaten when Mesut Özil looks to have time and space to shoot from outside the box, but instead the German plays a square pass to Alex Oxlade-Chamberlain who then tricks his way past four challenges on the edge of the box before finding the overlapping Nacho Monreal free, and the Spanish defender tucks the ball past compatriot David de Gea from the corner of the six-yard box to send the travelling Arsenal fans wild.

13 January 2016

In a breathless game at Anfield, the Gunners level the scores for the second time. Roberto Firmino has twice put Liverpool ahead but Arsenal again peg the hosts back with an Aaron Ramsey corner finding its way across the six-yard box until a hopeful prod by Olivier Giroud turns the ball past Simon Mignolet to make it 2-2.

26

21 December 1991

Ian Wright completes a 22-minute first-half hat-trick to put Arsenal 3-1 up against Everton. Apart from Wright's feat, Swedish right-winger Anders Limpar completes his own hat-trick – of assists – as he is once again sent clear down the right, latching on to Lee Dixon's pass, and as the goalkeeper comes out, Limpar guides the ball to his left for Wright to just get enough power on his shot to roll it into the bottom-right corner.

7 May 2003

Arsenal threaten to run up a cricket score against a shambolic Southampton at Highbury. The Gunners go 5-0 up as Jermaine Pennant marks a dream league debut as he completes an incredible nine-minute hat-trick. Pennant's goal is a result of more brilliance by Thierry Henry, who has been heavily involved in four of the five goals scored.

11 March 2004

A moment where Arsenal fans would welcome VAR, if it existed at that time! Playing Blackburn Rovers away at Ewood Park, Thierry Henry lurks with intent as Rovers keeper Brad Friedel prepares to kick the ball upfield. As the American drops the ball to volley it, Henry nicks it away, runs past and rolls the ball into the empty net. Referee Alan Wiley believes an infringement has occurred and Henry is nonplussed as he believes the ball had been in play the moment the keeper released it. TV pundits agree it should have stood and today, VAR would have a long check – but it is chalked off and the score remains 0-0 – for now.

5 February 2011

Robin van Persie puts the Gunners 4-0 up at St James' Park. As the saying goes, you could drive a proverbial bus through the porous Newcastle United defence and when Bacary Sagna's excellent cross into the box comes in, van Persie is unmarked and has all the time in the world to head powerfully home to increase the home fans' fury. With 64 minutes still to play, it seems a matter of how many goals Arsenal will score – but the Dutch striker's effort will be the last goal the Gunners manage and after later being reduced to ten men, Arsenal concede four goals in the space of 19 second-half minutes to throw away two vital points in a 4-4 draw.

30 October 2019

A young Arsenal side take a 2-1 lead in the Carabao Cup against Liverpool. Having fallen behind to an early own goal, Arsène Wenger's side show great character to bounce back quickly and Ainsley Maitland-Niles gets in behind the home defence, puts a dangerous cross into the six-yard box and Gabriel Martinelli eventually prods home following some poor defending by the home side.

27

5 December 2001

The Gunners go 2-0 up against Juventus at Highbury with a stunning Thierry Henry free kick. Already leading through a Freddie Ljungberg strike just six minutes earlier, Robert Pires is fouled just outside the box and a free kick is awarded. Despite the legendary Gianluigi Buffon organising the wall to his liking, Henry steps up and floats a 20-yard shot over the wall and into the top-left corner as if it was simplicity itself, with Buffon only able to stand and admire, though he stops short of applauding!

16 April 2004

The Gunners go 2-0 up against Leeds United with the pace of Thierry Henry too much for the visitors' defence. When Gilberto Silva nudges a pass into space behind the Leeds backline, Henry looks yards offside – but he's actually timed his run to perfection and with a clear run on goal he has the time to run from the right to a more central angle before nudging the ball past the keeper from close range.

9 January 2007

Jérémie Aliadière puts Arsenal ahead in what will be a classic League Cup quarter-final tie away to Liverpool. Kolo Touré spots Aliadière's clever diagonal run with a superb lofted pass and the French striker controls the ball before prodding it under the keeper and then finishing the job from a few yards out to put the Gunners 1-0 up at Anfield.

28

3 May 1998

Arsenal double their lead against Everton as the Gunners look for the three points that will confirm them as league champions. The second goal is worthy of winning any title. Emmanuel Petit robs John O'Kane and manages to slip the ball to Marc Overmars. The Dutch winger sprints at a retreating Everton defence and nudges the ball to the side of Dave Watson before hitting a powerful shot that the keeper gets a hand to but still goes over the line to make it 2-0.

29

7 January 2004

Patrick Vieira starts the move that leads to Arsenal taking the lead away to Everton. The combative midfielder receives the ball just inside the Toffees half before zipping a low pass to Freddie Ljungberg who, in turn, spots Nwankwo Kanu's dart into the box, and the Nigerian nips in ahead of David Unsworth before rounding keeper Nigel Martyn and rolling the ball home for his first league goal of the season.

18 January 2004

When it comes to brilliant improvisation and quick thinking, few in the game can top the genius of Thierry Henry, and his first goal against Aston Villa is the perfect example of that ingenuity. Awarded a free kick on the edge of the Villa box, Henry asks the referee if he is okay to take it quickly – the referee nods and while Villa are still organising their defensive wall, Henry calmly places a low shot around them and into the bottom corner to put the Gunners 1-0 up at Villa Park. Needless to add, the Villa players are furious with the official, but as harsh as it seems, the goal is within the laws of the game and stands.

30

5 April 1987

Arsenal fans fear the worst when Ian Rush gives Liverpool the lead after 23 minutes of the 1987 League Cup Final. Rush has never been on the losing side when he's scored for the Merseysiders – a run of 144 games – but the Gunners are level within seven minutes. Viv Anderson's cross sees Tony Adams's shot cleared as far as Charlie Nicholas, and the Scotland striker sees his low shot strike the foot of the post from close range. But Anderson is first to the rebound and his low cross back into the six-yard box is swept home by Nicholas to make it 1-1 and send one half of Wembley wild.

14 January 2006

José Antonio Reyes is the creator of Arsenal's third goal, with the Spaniard also claiming his second assist of the game. If his first assist has been standard fare (from a corner), this is sublime as he advances to the halfway line before sending a slide-rule pass into the path of Thierry Henry, who hits a low shot past the advancing Middlesbrough keeper Brad Jones that rolls into the bottom-right corner with unerring accuracy to make it 3-0.

31

8 April 2001

Trailing 1-0 in the FA Cup semi-final against Tottenham at Old Trafford, the Gunners draw level with a majestic header from the superb Patrick Vieira. Sol Campbell is deservedly booked by referee Graham Poll for a foul on Ray Parlour and the Spurs defender is forced off the pitch to receive treatment after injuring himself in the process. Campbell's absence from the resulting free kick is punished as Robert Pires's whipped cross from the right is glanced home by Vieira to give keeper Neil Sullivan no chance and make the score 1-1.

4 May 2003

Arsenal level in a game they can ill afford to lose against Leeds United. In a thrilling title race with Manchester United at the top of the Premier League, the Gunners have surprisingly fallen behind to a Harry Kewell goal before fighting back at a sun-drenched Highbury. Ray Parlour drives forward and then fires in a low shot that Leeds keeper Paul Robinson pushes up – but only on to the woodwork where the rebound is calmly headed home by Thierry Henry to make it 1-1.

4 October 2003

Arsenal survive another difficult test, this time at Anfield, where they trail from an early Harry Kewell strike. The equaliser has more than a fraction of good fortune about it as Robert Pires sends a dangerous free kick in from the right flank and Edu's header strikes Liverpool's Sami Hyypiä before rolling into the back of the net to draw the Gunners level.

10 February 2004

A landmark goal gives Arsenal a 1-0 lead at Highbury against Southampton. A typically fast counter-attack sees Robert Pires collect the ball on the halfway line before passing down the left to Thierry Henry. There is a hint of offside about the move, but Henry plays to the whistle, skipping past a challenge before firing a low shot that the keeper can't keep out of the net. It is Henry's 100th Premier League goal as his legendary status among Gunners fans continues to grow almost on a game-by-game basis.

9 April 2004

Having lost twice in a week – exiting the FA Cup and Champions League within the space of a few days – getting back to winning ways at home to Liverpool is crucial for the still unbeaten (in the Premier League) Gunners. Liverpool have gone ahead inside five minutes but Arsenal level when Robert Pires picks up a loose ball and chips a fine pass over to Thierry Henry, who takes one touch to control and then fires a low shot through the keeper's legs from 15 yards to make it 1-1. A crucial goal for a team whose mentality has been severely tested in recent days.

18 September 2004

Patrick Vieira is the driving force as Arsenal take the lead at Highbury against Bolton Wanderers. Vieira plays a ball forwards and is first to react as his own pass is cut out, then plays a more accurate pass into the path of Thierry Henry, who escapes the attention of two defenders before drilling a low shot past the keeper from 15 yards.

32

15 September 2019

Arsenal carve open the Watford defence to go 2-0 up. Mesut Özil plays a pass inside the Watford full-back for Ainsley Maitland-Niles to run on to and his low cross into the six-yard box is swept home by Pierre-Emerick Aubameyang at the far post for his second goal of the afternoon at Vicarage Road.

33

5 May 1999

Dennis Bergkamp's genius is again evident as Arsenal take a 2-0 lead at White Hart Lane in a must-win North London derby. Having already provided a sumptuous pass for Emmanuel Petit's opener, Bergkamp releases Nicolas Anelka with a pass that splits the Tottenham defence apart and Anelka races through to bury a shot past the keeper and put the Gunners on their way to three more crucial points.

11 May 2002

Everton complain long and loud that Dennis Bergkamp commits a foul in the build-up, but Arsenal's goal stands. Trailing 2-1, Bergkamp chases a ball down the left and tangles with an Everton defender who tumbles over and the now unchallenged Bergkamp then spots Thierry Henry's run, plays a simple ball into his path and the Frenchman tucks away a low shot to make it 2-2.

20 March 2003

Arsenal double their lead against Chelsea with a fine, flowing team move that has become the trademark of Arsène Wenger's exciting side. Sylvain Wiltord has been involved in the opening goal of the game just eight minutes earlier and this time, he is the scorer as Patrick Vieira finds the France striker on the edge of the box and his first-time low shot gives Carlo Cudicini no chance to silence Stamford Bridge and put Arsenal 2-0 up in the FA Cup quarter-final tie.

1 November 2003

It's all too easy for Arsenal, who go 3-0 up away to Leeds United with a third counter-attack goal in 33 minutes. This break begins with a Leeds corner and ends with Dennis Bergkamp firing a shot against the post from 18 yards and Thierry Henry sweeping home the rebound from ten yards for his second of the afternoon at Elland Road.

16 April 2004

Even Thierry Henry's penalties are a bit special as he proves yet again against Leeds United. Dennis Bergkamp plays a one-two with Sylvain Wiltord on the edge of the box and as the Dutch playmaker flicks the ball up over a Michael Duberry challenge, the Leeds defender makes a definite move to affect the trajectory with his elbow. The spot kick is awarded and Henry calmly dinks the ball over the keeper – 'Panenka' style – to make it 3-0 to the Gunners.

2 October 2004

Charlton Athletic's Jason Euell gives the ball away to Thierry Henry midway inside his own half and Henry immediately plays a low pass into the box towards Dennis Bergkamp, who chases it to the far right of the box and nips in ahead of the now stranded keeper – he looks up and plays a precise low ball into a crowded six-yard box that is swept home by Freddie Ljungberg to make it 1-0.

4 October 2009

Arsenal draw level for the second time of an open and entertaining first half against Blackburn Rovers at the Emirates. Trailing 2-1, the Gunners dissect the visitors' defence as Cesc Fàbregas plays a superb through ball to Robin van Persie on the edge of the box, and the Dutch striker takes the pass in his stride before rifling a low left-foot shot across the keeper and into the bottom corner to make it 2-2.

26 September 2015

Alexis Sánchez puts the Gunners 2-1 up at Leicester City. An attack down the right sees a low ball come into the six-yard box and it works its way to the far post where Sánchez – who has gone eight games without finding the back of the net – neatly tucks the ball in the bottom-left corner for his first of the season. The Foxes, who haven't won any of their previous 17 Premier League games against Arsenal, are once again finding the Gunners are kryptonite to their challenge, no matter how well they are playing.

21 December 2015

A stunning goal from Theo Walcott gives Arsenal the lead against Manchester City at the Emirates. Mesut Özil finds Walcott on the left of the City box and the former Southampton man cuts back out a yard before unleashing a powerful angled shot from 20 yards that flies into the top-right corner to put Arsenal 1-0 up against Manuel Pellegrini's side.

34

20 May 1993

Just as he has done seven days earlier, Ian Wright opens the scoring in the 1993 FA Cup Final – albeit a replay. Alan Smith glances on a long ball from defence into Wright's path and the Gunners striker uses his pace to get in behind the Sheffield Wednesday defence before deftly lifting the ball over goalkeeper Chris Woods from the edge of the box and into the net, despite the despairing attempts of two defenders.

6 April 1995

Arsenal take the lead against Sampdoria in the 1994/95 European Cup Winners' Cup semi-final first leg at Highbury. Ray Parlour attempts to trick his way into the box on the left but his overhead flick is cleared to the edge of the area, where David Hillier fires a powerful shot in that is saved by the keeper but tucked away by Steve Bould from eight yards out.

9 August 1998

Double winners Arsenal take on fierce rivals Manchester United at Wembley in the 1998 FA Charity Shield showdown. And it's the Gunners who strike first when Dennis Bergkamp's clever back-heel finds Nicolas Anelka who is challenged, and the ball runs free to Marc Overmars who lashes a shot high into the roof of the net from eight yards to make it 1-0.

35

29 March 1994

Arsenal grab a crucial away goal in the first leg of the European Cup Winners' Cup semi-final. In a hostile Parc des Princes, the Gunners win a free kick on the right of the Paris Saint-Germain box. Paul Davis floats in a free kick and as three Arsenal players compete for the ball, it is Ian Wright who connects as he glances a header into the bottom-left corner to make it 1-0. David Ginola levels for PSG after the break as the game ends 1-1.

13 April 2003

Arsenal score what proves to be the only goal of the FA Cup semi-final against Sheffield United at Old Trafford. The First Division outfit are left furious when a series of decisions go against them in the build-up to the goal that starts with referee Graham Poll waving play on after Wayne Allison seems to be fouled by Sol Campbell, before the official then accidently blocks an attempted challenge by Michael Tonge as Arsenal break forward. Undeterred, Francis Jeffers wriggles to the goal line and picks out Sylvain Wiltord, who sees his flicked effort hit the post from close range – but Wiltord quickly wins the ball back, crosses into the middle and Freddie Ljungberg makes no mistake, hitting his shot in off the underside of the crossbar. The decision not to stop play (VAR being many years away) sparks an angry reaction from Sheffield United and their manager Neil Warnock in particular, but the crucial goal stands and sends the Gunners into yet another major domestic final.

18 August 2003

Having been reduced to ten men after Sol Campbell's 25th-minute red card for a professional foul, the Gunners are given the opportunity to take the lead against Everton on the opening day of the 2003/04 season. Freddie Ljungberg carries the ball into the Everton half before cutting inside and lofting a pass into the right channel for Thierry Henry who delicately lifts the ball to move around Alan Stubbs, but the Everton defender appears to nudge the ball away with his elbow. A penalty is given and Henry calmly rolls the ball down the middle with former Gunners keeper Richard Wright wrong-footed to make it 1-0.

29 December 2003

Robert Pires scores his seventh goal in six meetings with Southampton but he has Thierry Henry to thank for what will also prove to be the winning goal at St Mary's Stadium. Henry heads a throw-in to Dennis Bergkamp who returns the pass to the France striker. Henry then moves purposefully towards the Saints box before playing an eye of the needle pass into the path of Pires on the right, and he finishes with a low shot across the keeper. The win means the Gunners have remained unbeaten since May – seven months without losing a game – incredible.

25 April 2004

Robert Pires instigates the move that puts Arsenal 2-0 up at White Hart Lane on a day Arsène Wenger's unbeaten side need just a point to clinch the Premier League title.

Pires finds Dennis Bergkamp who ups the ante with a ball into the box for Patrick Vieira, who cuts the ball back for Pires to steer into the corner of the net. It is enough to give the Gunners enough breathing space to take the point needed after Spurs rally for a 2-2 draw – but the dream scenario is complete as the title is confirmed on Tottenham soil in an unforgettable day for Arsenal fans who celebrate accordingly.

7 May 2006

Arsenal's final game at Highbury seems to be going wrong as Wigan Athletic recover from a goal down to lead 2-1 – but Thierry Henry levels ten minutes before the break with a typically precise finish. Having won possession back midway inside the Wigan half, the ball falls to Robert Pires who sends Henry clear and the French striker places a low shot past the keeper from the edge of the box to make it 2-2 – much to the relief of the home fans, desperate to see the old ground given a winning send-off.

36

9 October 1988

The Football League, celebrating its 100th year of existence, organises a tournament between eight clubs with the final to be played at Villa Park. Though the competition has a lukewarm reception from fans of the clubs involved, the Football League Centenary Trophy is a one-off tournament that Arsenal want to win. The sides that finished in the top eight in Division One the previous season compete and Arsenal see off Nottingham Forest and Liverpool to reach the final where Manchester United awaited the Gunners. Paul Davis puts Arsenal ahead with a smart left-foot volley from eight yards out.

6 April 1995

Arsenal score a second goal in the space of two minutes to go 2-0 up in the European Cup Winners' Cup semi-final first leg at Highbury. Stefan Schwarz sends in a corner that John Hartson flicks towards the back post, and Steve Bould beats Ian Wright to nod the ball down into the bottom-left corner of the Sampdoria net – it is central defender Bould's second goal of the game.

28 August 2004

Thierry Henry doubles the Gunners' lead at Carrow Road as a smart move again undoes the Norwich City defence. José Antonio Reyes finds Freddie Ljungberg, who exchanges passes with Henry before sending in a cross that Henry leaps to meet and nod home from six yards out.

17 May 2006

Arsenal take a dramatic lead through Sol Campbell in the 2006 Champions League Final against Barcelona. Despite being reduced to ten men following goalkeeper Jens Lehmann's sending off, it is Arsène Wenger's side who strike first against the Catalans with a towering header from Campbell after a free kick on the right of the box, giving keeper Víctor Valdés no chance and allowing thousands of Gunners fans to dare to dream of a famous victory ...

21 April 2009

Andrey Arshavin gives Arsenal the lead at Anfield on what is a very special night for the Russian forward on Merseyside. Samir Nasri nudges a pass into the path of Cesc Fabregas who pulls the ball back into the six-yard box, and Arshavin arrives with perfect timing to hit a fierce shot off the underside of the crossbar and into the Liverpool net to make it 1-0 for the Gunners.

29 October 2011

Robin van Persie levels the scores at Stamford Bridge after the Gunners have previously missed a host of chances. Frank Lampard puts Chelsea ahead, but Gervinho bursts through the hosts' defence before squaring to the unmarked van Persie who rolls the ball into the empty net and silences the majority of the 40,000+ crowd.

30 October 2019

Arsenal send their travelling fans into dreamland as Gabriel Martinelli makes it 3-1 for the Gunners in the Carabao Cup tie at Anfield. Bukayo Saka is again involved as he races down the left flank before sending a low ball into the middle to give Gabriel Martinelli the simplest of chances, and the Brazilian makes no mistake from close range to score his second of the evening and put the Gunners firmly in the driving seat against Jurgen Klopp's runaway Premier League leaders.

37

11 May 2005

A goal of great beauty puts Arsenal 3-0 up against Everton at Highbury. Robin van Persie receives a pass on the edge of the Everton box and lays it off to Dennis Bergkamp and his first-time poke leaves Patrick Vieira clear on goal, and the French powerhouse gently lifts the ball over Richard Wright and into the net to send Highbury wild. Breathtaking football by Arsène Wenger's men.

4 October 2009

Cesc Fabregas claims his second assist of the game as he finds Andrey Arshavin on the left, and the Russian drives into the box before skipping past Martin Olsson and lashing a rising shot past the keeper and into the top right of the net to put the Gunners 3-2 up against Blackburn Rovers at the Emirates.

29 October 2009

Arsenal get back on level terms against Tottenham in a thrilling North London derby at the Emirates. Having fallen behind to a spectacular David Bentley strike, it's a set piece that equalises for the hosts as Robin van Persie's corner finds the head of Mikaël Silvestre and the French defender guides the ball into the corner of the net to send the Gunners' fans wild.

18 August 2018

Having missed a good chance not long before, Henrikh Mkhitaryan makes no mistake with a more difficult opportunity as he pulls a goal back for the Gunners at Stamford Bridge. Chelsea have led 2-0, but when the ball falls to Mkhitaryan on the edge of the box he hits a powerful low shot past Kepa and into the bottom-left corner to halve the deficit.

38

23 December 1978

Arsenal double their lead at White Hart Lane with an excellent second goal for Alan Sunderland. Liam Brady plays a delightful crossfield pass to the feet of Sunderland who, alone, cuts in towards the box and three Spurs defenders – but none get near him in time as Sunderland unleashes a powerful left-foot shot into the same top-right corner his opening goal had gone into and gives the Gunners a 2-0 lead in the North London derby.

24 April 1999

Arsenal double their lead over Middlesbrough at the Riverside Stadium. It's a goal created by Patrick Vieira who picks up the ball inside his own half before embarking on a trademark driving run through the middle of the pitch, before playing a pass into the path of Nicolas Anelka who calmly hits a low shot through the onrushing Mark Schwarzer's legs and makes it 2-0 for the Gunners.

14 April 2002

Arsenal book a place in the FA Cup Final with a scrappy 1-0 victory over Middlesbrough at Old Trafford. Boro sub Gianluca Festa – who has only come on the pitch just seven minutes earlier – is in the wrong place at the wrong time as the Italian defender inadvertently wafts a foot at Thierry Henry's low corner and volleys the ball past his own keeper – Mark Schwarzer – and into the roof of the net from eight yards out to score what will be the only goal of the game. In truth, it was a fine finish!

17 May 2003

It proves to be sweet 16 for Arsenal who are appearing in their 16th FA Cup Final with Southampton the opposition at the Millennium Stadium in Cardiff. Far from a classic, the game is settled by a solitary goal from Robert Pires. Dennis Bergkamp finds Freddie Ljungberg in the Saints box and his effort is blocked and falls to Pires, who bundles the ball home from close range and ensures the Gunners retain the trophy they've won the season before and record another success in the competition the club loves.

10 January 2004

Arsenal are awarded a penalty after Robert Pires plays a pass to Patrick Vieira, who appears to be bundled over in the box by defender Ugo Ehiogu. The Middlesbrough protests are long and loud and when Thierry Henry squeezes the spot kick under keeper Mark Schwarzer, the France international's agitated celebration suggests the Boro players have been doing their best to put him off. Don't disturb a master at work!

39

19 October 1991

David Rocastle scores a wonderful goal against Manchester United at Old Trafford, though the sublime chip is later credited to a Peter Schmeichel own goal. Rocastle shimmies through two challenges with quick feet before spotting Schmeichel a few yards off his line – he chips the ball from 30 yards and as it sails over the Dane's head, it hits the crossbar, bounces out and hits the United goalkeeper's head and rebounds into the back of the net. Technically an own goal, but Rocky deserved it more.

11 May 2003

Arsenal punish bottom-of-the-table Sunderland's slack passing for the second time at the Stadium of Light with a swift counter-attack that sees a deep cross into the box find Thierry Henry's head, whose cushioned header is swept home by Freddie Ljungberg from close range to put the Gunners 2-0 up and very much in cruise control.

26 October 2003

Trailing 1-0 to Charlton Athletic it is Thierry Henry who preserves Arsenal's unbeaten start to the season with a stunning free kick at The Valley. Having already struck the post with a curling shot from the left not long before, Henry lines up a free kick from 20 yards out and curls the ball over the wall, over the keeper and into the top-right corner of the Addicks' net to make it 1-1 and secure a point in South London. A sublime free kick from a player at the very peak of his powers.

15 August 2004

Arsenal double their opening day lead away to Everton with a typically sweeping move. In the Merseyside sunshine, the Gunners make hay as José Antonio Reyes heads home after Freddie Ljungberg picks up a rare loose ball from Thierry Henry before taking on two defenders and crossing in from the left, where Reyes makes no mistake against a static home defence to make it 2-0 for the champions, who appear to have carried on where they left off the previous campaign.

40

9 October 1988

Arsenal increase their advantage over Manchester United in the Football League Centenary Trophy Final at Villa Park. Paul Davis, having given the Gunners the lead just four minutes earlier, plays a threaded pass through to Michael Thomas who drills a low shot through the United keeper and into the net to make it 2-0 in front of a disappointing but enthusiastic 22,182 crowd. Though United pull one back after the break, the Gunners hold firm to edge home 2-1 and ensure they will be the only winners of this one-off tournament.

23 December 2001

Arsenal have their 40th player sent off since Arsène Wenger became manager some five and a half years earlier. Referee Paul Durkin decides that Giovanni van Bronckhorst has dived in the box and as a result, dismisses the Dutch star by showing him a second yellow card during the clash with Liverpool at Anfield. With the score still 0-0, the advantage now appears to be firmly in Liverpool's favour ...

13 September 2003

Thierry Henry equalises from the penalty spot against Harry Redknapp's Portsmouth at Highbury. The visitors have gone ahead on 26 minutes when former Spurs striker Teddy Sheringham scores from close range but a slightly off-colour Gunners level before the break when Robert Pires is bundled over in the box and the referee awards a spot kick. Though Henry tucks the ball confidently home, the celebrations are cut short when the official orders a retake for an infringement. Henry again steps up, puts the ball in the opposite corner and makes it 1-1, and with no further scoring, Pompey end the Gunners' 100 per cent start to the 2003/04 Premier League campaign.

28 August 2004

Terrible defending by the hosts allows the free-scoring Gunners to go 3-0 up away to Norwich City. Robert Pires plays a short pass to Thierry Henry who chips what seems to be a poor cross into the Canaries box, but the defender's attempt to control the ball allows Freddie Ljungberg to poke it into Pires's path and he finishes with a low, angled shot.

9 January 2007

Júlio Baptista gets his first goal of what will be an unforgettable evening for the Brazilian forward. Level at 1-1 in the League Cup quarter-final with Liverpool, the Gunners are awarded a free kick 25 yards out. Baptista steps up to take the set piece and whips a shot over the wall and past a static Jerzy Dudek to make it 2-1 for the visitors.

26 February 2012

Bacary Sagna scores a rare goal to spark an Arsenal revival in the North London derby at the Emirates. Trailing 2-0 to a couple of rather fortuitous Spurs goals – a deflected Louis Saha shot and a questionable penalty won by Gareth Bale

– the Gunners desperately look for a goal before the break and it comes when Mikel Arteta dinks a chip towards the penalty spot and Sagna meets it on the full and buries a header past Brad Friedel.

30 May 2015

FA Cup holders Arsenal are looking for a 12th success in the competition when they return to Wembley to face Aston Villa just 12 months after seeing off Hull City in the final. Villa have stoically held out for most of the half until Theo Walcott breaks the deadlock just before half-time, as Nacho Monreal's cross finds the head of Alexis Sánchez and the Chilean's header back across goal finds Walcott, who thumps the ball emphatically past Shay Given to make it 1-0.

24 September 2016

Mesut Özil starts and finishes a devastating counter-attack that results in Arsenal taking a 3-0 first-half lead against Chelsea at the Emirates. The German playmaker spins away from N'Golo Kanté just outside his own box before racing upfield. With only two defenders and Alexis Sánchez for company, Özil slips a pass to Sánchez who lofts a return ball towards the back post and Özil volleys down into the ground, but the ball bounces over Thibaut Courtois and into the back of the net.

41

1 November 2016

Olivier Giroud heads home to make it 2-2 against Ludogorets in Bulgaria. The Gunners have trailed 2-0 after just 15 minutes but Granit Xhaka reduces the arrears on 20 minutes and Giroud equalises as he nods in Aaron Ramsey's clipped cross.

18 August 2018

Arsenal come back from being 2-0 down to level the scores at 2-2 just before the break. Henrikh Mkhitaryan, who has halved the deficit just four minutes earlier, is the provider, drifting out on the right of the Chelsea box before sending a low pinpoint cross to the right foot of Alex Iwobi, who uses the power of the pass to thump home past Kepa from seven yards out.

42

16 April 2005

With Arsenal equalling a record of five consecutive FA Cup semi-final appearances, Blackburn Rovers hold out until the 42nd minute at the Millennium Stadium as Robert Pires finally opens the scoring. Patrick Vieira's chip finds Kolo Touré at the back post and after outwitting Rovers defender Ryan Nelson, the Ivory Coast centre-back picks out Pires who taps in from close range.

7 November 2012

An opportunist goal by Lukas Podolski puts Arsenal 2-1 up against Spurs at the Emirates. Two Spurs players dither over a loose ball and Podolski nips in between them and fires a shot towards goal that takes a slight deflection and bobbles into the bottom corner of the net with the keeper wrong-footed.

10 August 2014

Arsenal double their lead against Manchester City in the 2014 FA Community Shield at Wembley. Alexis Sánchez finds Yaya Sanogo in the City box and his persistence leads to him playing a short pass to Aaron Ramsey, who takes the ball on a yard before hitting a low shot to the goalkeeper's right and makes it 2-0 just before the break.

19 December 2017

A much-changed Arsenal just edge past West Ham United in the Carabao Cup quarter-final at the Emirates.

The only goal of the game comes just before the break when a cross to the right of the West Ham box finds the head of Mathieu Debuchy who intelligently heads the ball across the six-yard box, and in the ensuing scramble, Danny Welbeck prods past Joe Hart for what will prove to be the winning goal and sets up an all-London two-legged semi-final with Chelsea.

43

12 May 1979

Arsenal score what seems to be a killer second goal just before half-time to go 2-0 up against Manchester United in the 1979 FA Cup Final at Wembley. The graceful Irish architect that is Liam Brady proves the creator as he skips past one challenge on the edge of the United box before gliding past another and picking out Frank Stapleton in the six-yard box, and the Irish striker makes no mistake with a trademark header into the bottom corner.

44

20 September 1998

Nicolas Anelka puts Arsenal 2-0 up against Manchester United at Highbury. Marc Overmars lofts a pass over the United defence and Anelka races clear, sees his first shot well saved by Peter Schmeichel but collects the rebound and tucks home into the bottom-left corner to double the lead over the Red Devils.

28 October 2000

Newly promoted Manchester City, who haven't won at Highbury for 24 years going into this game, have held their own against Arsenal for most of the first half. But when defender Danny Tiatto is sent off for a second bookable offence, the Gunners immediately punish the visitors from a free kick some 20 yards out. Dennis Bergkamp touches the ball to his left and Ashley Cole strikes a low shot that seems to catch goalkeeper Nicky Weaver by surprise and the ball hits the back of the net without the City custodian moving. It's cruel on City who (correctly) must fear the worst after two hammer blows when they have been so close to taking a commendable 0-0 scoreline in at the break.

26 February 2012

Arsenal stun Tottenham with a second goal in four minutes to go into the break at 2-2. The equaliser comes when a Gunners attack is partially cleared to the edge of the box where Robin van Persie collects the loose ball. The Dutch striker, facing away from goal, then spins around before firing a left-foot screamer into the top-left corner of the net to send the Emirates wild. It's the prolific van Persie's 29th goal of the campaign – with three months still remaining.

45

6 September 1913

George Jobey writes his name into club folklore by becoming the first Arsenal player to score at Highbury. Jobey rises to head home Tommy Winship's corner on the stroke of half-time and level the score with Leicester Fosse who have led from the 20th minute. Jobey, making his home debut after signing for Arsenal, will also claim another notable first in the second home game as he will then become the first player to be stretchered off injured at Highbury and be later taken home on a milkman's cart, proving how quickly football can turn sour!

12 October 1953

Trailing 1-0 to a goal from Blackpool's Stan Mortensen in the FA Charity Shield clash at Highbury, the Gunners level the score just on half-time. Right-winger Cliff Holton dispossesses Seasiders defender Eddie Shimwell and his cross finds Tommy Lawton, who scores from an acute angle to make it 1-1.

2 May 1981

Arsenal go 2-0 up against Aston Villa at Highbury. Pat Jennings punches a corner clear and Peter Nicholas hoofs the ball towards the halfway line where Brian McDermott carries the ball towards the box. Despite the presence of two Villa defenders, he beats one, shoots between the legs of another and the ball somehow finds its way into the bottom corner of the net. A strange, but welcome, goal that will secure a European spot for the Gunners and, despite the loss, the 10,000 or so travelling Villa fans get to celebrate a first top-flight title since 1910, with close rivals Ipswich Town losing away to Middlesbrough.

14 April 1991

Arsenal pull a goal back just before the break in the FA Cup semi-final at Wembley. Trailing 2-0 to Tottenham, the Gunners are finally thrown a lifeline when Lee Dixon's deep cross from the right flank holds up slightly in the wind for Alan Smith to rise and head the ball into the bottom corner and halve the deficit – though Spurs will go on to win 3-1 in a desperately disappointing North London derby for Arsenal supporters.

21 September 1997

Dennis Bergkamp equalises for the Gunners away to Chelsea. Having fallen behind just five minutes earlier to a Gus Poyet goal, Patrick Vieira drives Arsenal forward and his pass finds Ian Wright who cushions a header into the path of Bergkamp, who coolly slots the ball under the keeper to send the teams in level at the break.

24 April 1999

Arsenal grab a third on the stroke of half-time to go 3-0 up at Middlesbrough's Riverside Stadium. It is started and finished by Nwankwo Kanu, who spins off a challenge on the right flank before cutting in and playing the ball to Nicolas Anelka on the right of the Boro box – his low cross is then collected by Kanu who takes the slightest of touches to take it away from the defender before slotting a low shot into the bottom-right corner – and this against a side who has lost just one of their previous 36 home games.

14 January 2006

Arsenal bag a fourth goal just before the half-time whistle to effectively seal three points. Middlesbrough allow Robert Pires too much room as he weighs up his options before lofting a clever chip over Brad Jones to make it 4-0 at the break.

First-half stoppage time

45+1

16 October 2004

Arsenal slice Aston Villa apart with a move that rarely deviates from the centre of the pitch. Starting in defence, the move cuts through the Villa midfield and José Antonio Reyes then splits the defence with a ball into the path of Thierry Henry, who races clear before drilling a low shot past the keeper to lead 2-1 at Highbury.

13 November 2004

Thierry Henry scores Arsenal's equaliser in what will prove to be an unforgettable North London derby at White Hart Lane. Trailing 1-0 to a 37th-minute Noureddine Naybet volley, the Gunners level in first-half added time. Lauren's superb ball from the right flank finds Henry, who controls the ball superbly before prodding home from eight yards to make it 1-1.

9 January 2007

Alex Song Billong puts Arsenal 3-1 up at Anfield in the League Cup quarter-final with Liverpool with a somewhat fortuitous goal from close range. The Gunners defender challenges as a corner comes in and as Sami Hyypiä attempts to clear the ball, it hits Song and flies past Jerzy Dudek to give the Gunners a two-goal advantage on the stroke of half-time. Nobody in yellow is complaining!

7 November 2012

Olivier Giroud slides home Arsenal's third goal of the first half against Tottenham to send the Emirates wild. The goal is created by Santi Cazorla who rides a couple of challenges on the left before crossing low into the middle, where Giroud sweeps home at the near post.

21 December 2015

Arsenal double their advantage over Manchester City in first-half stoppage time. Mesut Özil claims his second assist of the game as he drives towards the City penalty area before slipping a pass into the path of Olivier Giroud who hits a low, angled shot through the legs of Joe Hart to make it 2-0 at the Emirates. The Gunners go on to claim all three points despite a spectacular late goal from Yaya Touré.

23 November 2016

Arsenal again are forced to come from behind in the return Champions League group stage clash with Paris Saint-Germain at the Emirates. Mesut Özil feeds Alexis Sánchez who is then tripped by PSG's Grzegorz Krychowiak and the referee awards a penalty. Olivier Giroud steps up to convert and make it 1-1 in first-half stoppage time.

45+2

23 December 2001

Ten-man Arsenal take the lead at Anfield after Thierry Henry strokes home a penalty in front of the Kop. Nwankwo Kanu is the architect, threading a pass into Freddie Ljungberg who is brought down by Liverpool keeper Jerzy Dudek, giving the referee no other option but to point to the spot. Henry strokes the penalty into the bottom-left corner to end the half on a high.

10 January 2004

Arsenal take a 2-0 lead with a second goal in nine minutes against Middlesbrough. Thierry Henry's free kick towards the far post results in Boro defender Franck Queudrue lunging to clear, but he only manages to poke the ball past his own keeper from close range.

9 January 2007

Júlio Baptista completes a remarkable first half for Arsenal as he makes it 4-1 at Anfield in the League Cup quarter-final against Liverpool. It is the Gunners' third goal in less than seven minutes and all but secures victory, with the on-fire Baptista skipping past two challenges before slipping a ball to his left where Jérémie Aliadière is deemed to be onside, and the Frenchman returns the pass to Baptista who makes no mistake from six yards out to leave Anfield suitably stunned.

30 October 2012

Theo Walcott begins one of the most amazing comebacks in Arsenal's long, proud history. The Capital One Cup fourth-round tie away to Reading has been anything but proud for the shambolic Gunners who have gone 4-0 down at the Madejski Stadium with only 36 minutes played. In first-half stoppage time, the unlikeliest of recoveries begins as Andrey Arshavin plays a slide-rule ball through to Walcott who races in between two defenders, before coolly dinking it over the onrushing Royals keeper Adam Federici.

45+4

8 March 2018

Aaron Ramsey puts the Gunners in the driving seat with a second goal in first-half stoppage time. After dominating the first half against AC Milan, the Gunners put one foot in the Europa League quarter-finals with a second goal at the San Siro. Ramsey collects Mesut Özil's threaded pass through the centre of Milan's defence and takes the ball around keeper Gianluigi Donnarumma to tap home and secure what will be a 2-0 victory over the Italians.

The second half ...

46

29 October 2009

Arsenal go 2-1 up against Spurs and just as the first goal, it is a set piece headed home by a defender that undoes Spurs. Robin van Persie whips a free kick into the box from the right flank and William Gallas rises to nod the ball home from eight yards out as the Gunners once again expose the visitors' soft centre.

47

27 March 1971

Peter Storey gives Arsenal a lifeline in the FA Cup semi-final against Stoke City at Sheffield Wednesday's Hillsborough. The Gunners have found themselves 2-0 down after just 30 minutes against the Potters but start the second period in the best possible fashion, as a goalmouth scramble sees the ball fall to Storey who thumps a powerful shot goalwards that takes a sizeable deflection before ending up in the bottom-right corner of Gordon Banks's net.

31 March 1971

The Gunners go 2-0 up against Stoke City at Villa Park with a goal just after the start of the second half of the FA Cup semi-final replay. The move that leads to the goal starts with Gordon Armstrong passing the ball to John Radford on the left, and his low cross is missed by a couple of Stoke defenders and finds its way to Ray Kennedy who deftly lifts the ball into the right corner of the net from six yards out. It will be enough to send Arsenal to a first FA Cup Final since 1952.

15 April 1972

There is an incredible twist of fate involved in Arsenal's opening goal of the 1972 FA Cup semi-final against Stoke City. The two teams have met at the same stage the previous season, with the Gunners triumphing after a replay, so to face each other again is not what either side has hoped for when the draw is made. But the quirk is in the timing as this will be the third time in three successive FA Cup semi-finals against Stoke that Arsenal score in the 47th minute – clearly, the Potters weren't learning to be alert just after the restart! The Gunners attack with a ball into the Stoke box which is partially cleared into the air. Charlie George hopefully leaps with a defender and manages to head the ball back to the edge of the box where George Armstrong arrows a volley past the keeper and into the right of the net from 20 yards to put Arsenal ahead at Villa Park.

7 May 2003

Arsenal declare at six against Southampton when Robert Pires completes his hat-trick just two minutes after the restart with a superb 25-yard chip over the stranded Paul Jones. Pires and Jermaine Pennant both have three goals in the game with the scoring oddly stopping despite a 6-1 lead for Arsène Wenger's men. Though nobody realises it at the time, this victory is the first of a record-breaking 49-match unbeaten Premier League run and the birth of 'The Invincibles'.

15 May 2004

An historic day that few will forget as Arsenal look to complete the 2003/04 season without losing a game. Former Gunners player Paul Dickov has given Leicester City a first-half lead but just two minutes after the restart, Ashley Cole is bundled over in the box by a clumsy challenge and Henry drills home his 39th goal of an unforgettable season and makes the score 1-1.

21 February 2006

An historic night for the Gunners who become the first English team to beat Real Madrid at the Bernabeu. Arsenal go looking for the early goal that will put them in command of the Champions League round of 16 tie but spurn several early chances against Los Blancos. But just after the restart, Thierry Henry scores a goal that is worthy of the stage as he picks up the ball just inside his own half before moving forward and leaving three Madrid players with one burst of acceleration, and as Sergio Ramos moves across to challenge the French striker, Henry buries a low shot past Iker Casillas to score what will be the only goal of the game.

48

28 September 1991

Nigel Winterburn wins the ball just inside his own half before cutting in and playing a low pass into the path of Ian Wright, making his First Division debut, who accelerates to the edge of the box before firing an angled low shot into the bottom left-hand corner from 18 yards to put the Gunners 2-0 up against Southampton at The Dell.

31 August 2003

Arsenal level the scores away to Manchester City. Trailing from a bizarre first-half own goal from Lauren, the Gunners attack down the left and the advanced Ashley Cole receives the ball in the City penalty area, slides it across the six-yard box and Sylvain Wiltord beats former Gunners legend David Seaman to the ball and slides home the equaliser.

2 October 2004

The king of improvisation at his very best – Thierry Henry puts Arsenal 2-0 up against Charlton Athletic with the sort of goal only he seems capable of. When José Antonio Reyes finds Henry on the edge of the six-yard box, his marker is doing everything in his power to stop him turning – so Henry decides to back-heel the ball through the defender's legs and into the bottom-left corner of the net. Genius.

49

25 November 2003

Arsenal go back in front against Inter Milan in the San Siro. Having been pegged back in the first half, Freddie Ljungberg makes it 2-1 for the Gunners in the Champions League group stage clash, as Thierry Henry turns the full-back inside out before picking out the Swedish forward who controls the ball before knocking it past the keeper from close range.

9 April 2004

Robert Pires brings Arsenal level for the second time in the game in a tense battle with Liverpool. Thierry Henry plays a pass in from the left flank for Freddie Ljungberg and his first-time ball to Pires allows the France winger a clear view on goal. He makes no mistake from close range to make it 2-2.

29 October 2011

André Santos enjoys a rare moment of joy in an Arsenal shirt as he makes it 2-2 at Stamford Bridge. The Brazilian bursts down the left flank, runs into the space the narrow Chelsea defence has allowed and then drills a low shot home from just inside the box.

50

1 November 2003

Arsenal exact some payback on Leeds United who have twice played a huge role in denying the Gunners the title in recent years. The fourth goal for Arsène Wenger's men comes when a deep cross from the right goes to the left of the Leeds box where Robert Pires collects and picks out Gilberto Silva in the middle, who finishes with a low drive past Paul Robinson. Arsenal end the game 4-1 victors and, as a result, remain unbeaten in the first 13 games of the 2003/04 Premier League campaign.

8 August 2004

Gilberto Silva puts Arsenal 1-0 up in the 2004 FA Community Shield at Cardiff's Millennium Stadium. In the by now standard bad-tempered contest with Manchester United, the Gunners have missed numerous opportunities to take the lead – including an astonishing miss by José Antonio Reyes, who has slalomed his way through the United defence and around keeper Tim Howard before firing wide of the empty goal – but Reyes soon makes amends. Dennis Bergkamp threads a through ball into the Spaniard's path and Gilberto Silva races from midfield to collect Reyes's square pass and fire home from six yards out.

28 March 2004

Arsenal take the lead against Manchester United at Highbury with a special goal – even by Thierry Henry's standards. Henry collects the ball midway inside the United half and seems to have little else in his mind but to shoot for goal, and from 30 yards he hits a thunderous shot that swerves wickedly in mid-flight and totally bamboozles Roy Carroll in goal to put the Gunners 1-0 up. Though United will level late on, it means Arsenal are 32 matches unbeaten in the 2003/04 campaign and break the records previously set by Leeds United and Liverpool, while equalling the longest unbeaten run within a season set by Burnley some 83 years earlier.

9 April 2004

If this isn't Thierry Henry's best goal for the club, it is up there with some of his most sublime efforts in red and white. Having just levelled to make it 2-2 with Liverpool, Henry drives towards the box, dancing around Dietmar Hamann before being faced with a cluster of three defenders. With one drop of the shoulder he ghosts past all three to leave him facing the keeper and he is never going to miss from close range, sliding a low shot to send Highbury into raptures. A goal that sums up the magnificent season he is having. Henry's second of the game puts the Gunners ahead for the first time at 3-2 – though he wasn't quite finished yet in this game ...

16 April 2004

A lovely counter-attack goal that slices through Leeds United like a knife through butter. As a clearance falls to Dennis Bergkamp on the edge of his own box, he calmly chests a pass to Gilberto Silva who drives forward to the halfway line and then sends Thierry Henry clear – he sprints towards goal and then slides a low drive from the edge of the box to complete yet another hat-trick and put the Gunners 4-0 up. As a result, Henry became the first Arsenal player to hit back-to-back Highbury hat-tricks since Doug Lishman in 1951 – quite a feat.

4 May 2004

José Antonio Reyes preserves Arsenal's unbeaten season with a goal five minutes into the second half away to Portsmouth. With only three games remaining, the Gunners have gone in at the break at Fratton Park 1-0 down, but after Thierry Henry sees a shot thunder off the underside of the crossbar just after the restart, the same player is then heavily involved in the equalising goal a few minutes later. Henry toys with the Pompey right-back before sending a cross into the box that is headed clear, but only as far as Reyes who hits a crisp low volley past the keeper from 18 yards and earns a 1-1 draw.

25 August 2004

Thierry Henry nips in between Blackburn Rovers defenders Craig Short and Lucas Neill to put the Gunners 1-0 up at Highbury. Looking to set a new all-time league unbeaten run, emphatically, Henry converts Dennis Bergkamp's clever cross to finally break down a dogged Rovers defence.

11 May 2005

Arsenal go 4-0 up against Everton as Robert Pires drills home from close range. The three previous goals have all been the result of Dennis Bergkamp brilliance and though he is involved in the build-up, it is actually a Thierry Henry flick that hits Everton's Lee Carsley and bounces into

Pires's path and he makes no mistake with his second of the afternoon.

29 December 2012

Arsenal regain the lead against Newcastle United at the Emirates. The visitors have levelled Theo Walcott's opener just before the break, but Alex Oxlade-Chamberlain restores the advantage when he collects a poor clearance just outside the box and then drills a powerful low drive into the bottom-left corner to make it 2-1 to the Gunners.

30 May 2015

Having taken the lead five minutes before the break in the 2015 FA Cup Final against Aston Villa, the Gunners double their lead just five minutes after the restart with a spectacular goal from Alexis Sánchez. Receiving the ball midway inside the Villa half, Sánchez, with space and time, unleashes a howitzer of a shot that swerves and dips under the crossbar and into the back of the net, leaving Villa keeper Shay Given looking totally bemused.

51

12 October 1996

Arsenal go 2-0 up at Ewood Park with a classic counter-attacking goal. Patrick Vieira brings the ball forward before playing a clever pass with the outside of his foot – the ball lands at the feet of Ian Wright whose first touch takes him to the edge of the Blackburn Rovers box and as the keeper rushes out, Wright slides and hits a thunderous shot into the top-left corner of the net. It's his eighth of the season and with no further scoring, it is the perfect start for new manager Arsène Wenger.

26 February 2012

A third Arsenal goal in 11 minutes puts the Gunners 3-2 up against Spurs. Tomáš Rosický drives towards the Spurs box before laying a pass to his left for Bacary Sagna, who sends in a low ball to the near post where Rosicky arrives first to flick the ball past Brad Friedel.

52

26 May 1989

Needing to win by two clear goals to overtake Liverpool at the top of the First Division, Arsenal travel to Anfield as title underdogs. After keeping the home side out for the first half, the Gunners begin to take more risks and seven minutes after the break, Alan Smith opens the scoring. Nigel Winterburn's free kick finds the head of Smith who glances it past Bruce Grobbelaar to put Arsenal on the way to what will be an incredible victory. The Liverpool players insist Smith didn't touch the ball but the referee waves the protests away and the goal stands.

9 December 2000

Nwankwo Kanu gets the goal his overall performance deserves to put Arsenal 3-0 up at Highbury against Newcastle United. The move that leads to the goal starts with an excellent long ball from Freddie Ljungberg into Kanu's path, and the Nigerian takes one touch before flicking a low shot that goes past Shay Given and rolls inside the right post to put the game beyond Sir Bobby Robson's side with less than an hour played.

23 December 2001

Down to ten men, Arsenal take a 2-0 lead over Liverpool at Anfield. Robert Pires races down the left flank before playing a superb cross towards the near post, where Freddie Ljungberg nips in to side-foot the ball into the back of the net to give the Gunners a deserved second. Though Liverpool pull one back shortly after, Arsène Wenger's men hold on to win 2-1 – a first victory at Anfield for nine years and the first goals in this fixture for six years!

19 May 2013

Laurent Koscielny scores the goal that guarantees Arsenal a 16th successive season of Champions League football and condemns Tottenham to fifth spot and Europa League football. The winner comes when Theo Walcott's free kick is headed first by Lukas Podolski, then acrobatically hooked home by Koscielny from close range for what will be the only goal of a tense game at St James' Park. The match is a complete contrast to the ten-goal feast at the Emirates earlier in the season that the Gunners win 7-3. It also completes a superb run-in for Arsène Wenger's side who have won 12, drawn three and lost just one of the final 16 Premier League games. Moreover, it completes an 18th consecutive season Arsenal have finished above Spurs in the Premier League.

53

28 September 1991

Ian Wright scores his second of the game and Arsenal's third to go 3-0 up against Southampton at The Dell. Alan Smith cushions a long ball to his left and Wright scampers towards the box before tucking a low shot under the keeper to score his second in five minutes.

5 April 1997

David Platt puts the Gunners firmly in control of the London derby against Chelsea at Stamford Bridge. Leading 1-0 thanks to Ian Wright's first-half effort, Platt doubles Arsenal's advantage after Dennis Bergkamp splits the home defence apart again with a superb pass that releases Wright, and his low cross into the middle is converted by the England midfielder from close range.

22 February 2003

Arsenal wrap up three points at Maine Road before even an hour of the game is played. In truth, it has probably been won after 19 minutes when the Gunners have ripped a poor home defence to shreds and gone 4-0 up – the *coup de grâce* is yet to come, however, as the rampant Gunners go 5-0 up against Manchester City. Patrick Vieira picks up the ball and, from the halfway line, plays a pass to Dennis Bergkamp before continuing his run. Of course, the Dutch genius plays the perfect return ball into his path and as City's defence parts accordingly, Vieira runs clear before slotting a low shot past Nicky Weaver in goal to put the Gunners 5-0 up in what will be the last visit to Maine Road before it closes its doors for the final time later that summer.

18 January 2004

Thierry Henry scores from the spot – his second goal of the afternoon – to put Arsenal 2-0 up at Villa Park. The penalty is awarded after a brilliant piece of skill by Nwankwo Kanu, who uses his trickery to go past three defenders but as he passes the last – Olof Mellberg – he is tugged back for a clear foul. Henry fires the ball into the top-right corner of Thomas Sorensen's net and then has words with the Danish keeper, with the Arsenal striker clearly angry at something that has been said or done before he took it.

19 August 2006

Arsenal officially begin life at the Emirates Stadium with a Premier League clash against Aston Villa. Just as had happened in Highbury's first competitive game, it is the visitors who have the honour of scoring the first goal at the Gunners' new home and in this instance, Villa's Olof Mellberg writes a page in history as he heads home a corner to give the Midlands side a surprise 1-0 lead.

29 March 2014

Arsenal's slender title hopes take another blow as Manchester City claim a 1-1 draw at the Emirates. Needing a win to stay in touch with Chelsea, Liverpool and City, the Gunners trail to an early David Silva goal but level after the break when Mathieu Flamini sweeps home Lukas Podolski's cross into the box, giving Joe Hart no chance and earning the Gunners a share of the spoils which, on this occasion, is not enough.

54

15 August 2004

Everton are the masters of their own downfall as Arsenal go 3-0 up at Goodison Park on the opening day of the 2004/05 campaign. Joseph Yobo's lazy pass is intercepted by Dennis Bergkamp who feeds the ball wide to Thierry Henry and his cross is converted at close range by Freddie Ljungberg. All too easy for the Gunners.

22 August 2004

After Jimmy Floyd Hasselbaink and Franck Queudrue strikes have put Middlesbrough 3-1 up at Highbury, the Gunners' hopes of matching Nottingham Forest's long unbeaten league record of 42 games look set to end – but Dennis Bergkamp starts a remarkable comeback as he is allowed to advance with the ball towards the Boro penalty area before drilling a precise low drive into the bottom-left corner to reduce the arrears to one goal.

30 October 2019

Arsenal restore a two-goal advantage at Anfield after a defensive mix-up by Liverpool gifts the Gunners their fourth goal of the evening in a thrilling Carabao Cup tie. Ainsley Maitland-Niles capitalises on a short back pass to nick it past the keeper but across goal – but a quick-thinking Mesut Özil keeps the ball in play with a clever back-flick to give Maitland-Niles the simplest of chances that he duly tucks home to make it 4-2 and send 6,000 travelling fans into raptures.

55

19 April 1972

Arsenal equalise from the spot to make it 1-1 in the FA Cup semi-final replay with Stoke at Goodison Park. The decision to award a foul by Peter Dobing on George Armstrong as the Potters defender runs into the Arsenal man's back proves a highly controversial one, but Charlie George steps up to confidently fizz a low shot past Gordon Banks and level the scores.

8 May 2002

Having beaten Chelsea 2-0 to win the FA Cup just four days earlier, Arsenal travel to Old Trafford looking for the victory that will secure the Premier League title and complete the coveted 'double'. With United out of the running and Liverpool hoping for the Gunners to slip up, Arsène Wenger's side, unbeaten away all season, score the goal that confirms the title on 55 minutes with Sylvain Wiltord making his 100th appearance in style. United's Mikaël Silvestre gifts possession to Wiltord, who finds Freddie Ljungberg's driving run and after beating Laurent Blanc, he forces a save from Fabien Barthez – but only as far as Wiltord, who finishes from close range with a smart left-foot finish to ensure the Premier League crown is heading back to North London to cap another wonderful season for the imperious Gunners.

22 July 2004

Thierry Henry becomes the first Arsenal player to score at the Gunners' new home, the Emirates Stadium. It is an unofficial stat, as the game against Ajax is Dennis Bergkamp's testimonial with a crowd of 54,000 paying homage to the Dutch legend. It is entirely fittng that he plays a part in the goal that makes it 1-1 against Ajax, feeding Lee Dixon who in turn finds Henry who side-foots home at the near post to level the scores.

13 November 2004

A comedy of errors leads to Arsenal taking a 2-1 lead against Tottenham at White Hart Lane. Keeper Paul Robinson's attempted throw-out hits Ledley King and from the resulting confusion, Freddie Ljungberg beats Noé Pamarot who hauls down the Swede inside the box – Lauren steps up to convert the penalty, though the scoring in this game is far from finished.

29 October 2011

Arsenal go 3-2 up at Stamford Bridge thanks to an amazing piece of skill by Theo Walcott. Surrounded by four Chelsea players, Walcott somehow manages to wriggle clear of everyone around him to race into the box and fire a low shot inside Petr Cech's near post.

13 January 2016

Olivier Giroud grabs his 18th goal of the season to give the Gunners the lead for the first time in a thrilling encounter at Anfield. The Premier League leaders go 3-2 up when the ball arrives at the feet of Giroud eight yards out – the French striker spins off his marker before drilling a low shot into the bottom-left corner of the net. A late equaliser will deny Arsenal victory in yet another Anfield goal fest between the clubs.

56

7 May 2006

Having led 2-1 in Arsenal's final Highbury game, Wigan Athletic once again find themselves behind against the Gunners. The visitors, having had a clear penalty denied and missing two good chances, are the architects of their own downfall as David Thompson elects to work his way towards his own goal before stroking a woeful back pass and allowing Thierry Henry the opportunity of skipping past the keeper and calmly walking the ball into the net to put the Gunners 3-2 ahead.

2 December 2018

Trailing 2-1 after a controversial first-half penalty award by Mike Dean, Arsenal equalise against Spurs with a stunning goal from Pierre-Emerick Aubameyang. Héctor Bellerín plays a long, low pass from his own half and second-half sub Aaron Ramsey manages to help the ball inside to Aubameyang, who cracks an unstoppable drive from 18 yards with the keeper not even moving to send the Emirates wild.

57

3 May 1998

Marc Overmars all but seals the title with his second goal of the game to put Arsenal 3-0 up against Everton at Highbury. The Dutch forward uses his electric pace to create himself an opportunity which he duly converts with an angled shot across Toffees keeper Thomas Myhre into the far corner.

9 August 1998

Arsenal take a 2-0 lead over Manchester United in the FA Charity Shield clash at Wembley. Sub Christopher Wreh has replaced Dennis Bergkamp at the break and when he receives the ball on the edge of the United box, his low shot is saved by Peter Schmeichel – but the ball goes straight back to Wreh who tries the same shot again from the edge of the box and this time it finds the back of the net. Cue somersault celebration!

27 August 2003

In a feisty encounter at Highbury, Arsenal finally find a way past a stubborn Aston Villa defence. A Robert Pires corner is volleyed towards his own goal by Jlloyd Samuel, hitting the woodwork before bouncing back into the six-yard box where Sol Campbell powers a header into the back of the net from close range to make it 1-0.

20 December 2003

Arsenal's mini blip continues with a 1-1 draw at Bolton Wanderers and a third draw in four games. More worryingly, the free-scoring Gunners will have only scored three goals in four games after this match, where they initially lead through Robert Pires's scrappy goal. Dennis Bergkamp sends Thierry Henry away down the right – he plays it to Freddie Ljungberg whose shot is saved, and Pires scuffs the ball home from close range.

10 January 2004

Robert Pires starts and finishes the move that puts the Gunners 3-0 up at home to Middlesbrough. After winning the ball just outside the Boro box, he feeds Thierry Henry on the right and his low cross is miscued by Gareth Soughgate and Pires, who has continued his run, is presented with a simple chance which he duly takes with a low drive past Mark Schwarzer. It is Pires's ninth goal in 16 games.

11 March 2004

When Arsenal need a bit of magic to unlock a stubborn defence, inevitably it is provided by Thierry Henry – and that is the case on this occasion. The Gunners had lost 2-0 at Ewood Park the season before as the title hopes of Arsène Wenger's men began to come off the rails – and with the score still 0-0, Rovers are again proving difficult opposition on their own patch. Then, a free kick around 22 yards from goal – only one man is going to take it and Henry steps up and curls a perfect shot into the top-left corner of Brad Friedel's net for his 30th of the campaign.

4 October 2009

The outstanding Cesc Fàbregas puts Arsenal 4-2 up against Blackburn Rovers with a stunning goal. As an attack is half cleared, Tomáš Rosický loops the ball back over his head towards the edge of the box where Fàbregas hits a volley with the outside of his boot that flashes into the top-left corner of the net to give the Gunners the breathing space their overall performance merits.

26 September 2015

Arsenal open up a 3-1 lead at the King Power Stadium. The Gunners probe around the edge of the Leicester City box and the ball finds its way to Mesut Özil, who delicately chips a cross towards the penalty spot and Alexis Sánchez leaps to just get enough power and send the ball over Kasper Schmeichel and into the roof of the net.

58

21 September 1997

Dennis Bergkamp scores his second of the game to put Arsenal 2-1 up at Stamford Bridge. The goal is a result of some comedy defending by Chelsea as Michael Duberry slices a clearance before then trying to head the ball away, colliding with Frank Leboeuf, and the weak clearance lands at the feet of Bergkamp who sweeps a low shot home from 15 yards.

24 April 1999

A lovely move that has Arsenal's free-flowing attacking football stamped all over it. It starts with Nicolas Anelka playing a quick one-two on the halfway line and the return pass means he streaks clear of the Middlesbrough defence. Anelka weighs up his options before picking out Marc Overmars who nudges it on to Patrick Vieira, who calmly slots home from six yards to give the Gunners a 4-0 lead at the Riverside Stadium.

28 October 2000

Arsenal double their lead at Highbury against a ten-man Manchester City. Defender Laurent Charvet's poor clearance only finds Freddie Ljungberg who heads towards the City box before back-heeling the ball into the path of Dennis Bergkamp, who immediately sends a curling right-foot shot into the bottom-right corner and makes it 2-0 for the Gunners.

18 August 2003

It is a case of fourth time lucky as Arsenal double their lead at Highbury against Everton. Leading 1-0 but down to ten men, the vital second goal comes after several attempts on goal, including a scuffed effort from Patrick Vieira and a fierce drive from Thierry Henry, before Vieira has another wayward attempt that ends at the feet of Robert Pires who tucks the ball home from close range.

7 February 2004

Having been pegged back to 1-1 by Wolves at Molineux, the Gunners regain the advantage with a lovely finish from Thierry Henry. After a brief spell of keep ball, Robert Pires passes into the path of Henry who just gets there before the keeper, and he sends in a deft low shot that trickles over the line for his 99th Premier League goal for the club.

8 August 2004

Dennis Bergkamp plays a dangerous ball into the box from the right and the United defence fail to clear their lines – the ball breaks for José Antonio Reyes, who buries a low shot past Tim Howard and into the bottom-left corner to restore the Gunners' lead just minutes after United have made it 1-1 in the Community Shield clash at Cardiff.

25 August 2004

Cesc Fàbregas becomes Arsenal's youngest-ever scorer in the Premier League with a goal from perhaps an inch or so out! Thierry Henry's corner is powerfully headed towards goal by Gilberto Silva and – almost on the goal line – the ball hits Fàbregas's knee before going into the net. Fortunately, two Rovers defenders were either side of him and so there was no offside flag raised as the Gunners go 2-0 up and edge ever closer to a record unbeaten run.

9 January 2007

Jérémie Aliadière wins a penalty as Arsenal are given the chance to all but seal a place in the League Cup quarter-final. Theo Walcott slips the ball to the French striker and Sami Hyypiä brings him down in the box, and the referee points to the spot. Júlio Baptista steps up but sees his spot kick pushed away by Dudek and his chance of a hat-trick put on hold.

59

14 January 2006

Arsenal continue the rout against Middlesbrough when Gilberto Silva gets in on the act to make it 5-0 at Highbury with an hour still not on the clock. The Brazilian is allowed far too much space as Thierry Henry's free kick is floated in and he makes no mistake with a downward header from six yards out.

60

20 April 1995

Ian Wright bags a crucial equaliser to restore Arsenal's aggregate lead over Sampdoria and make it 1-1 on the night. John Hartson flicks a corner towards the back post and Wright forces the ball home from close in to give the Gunners the edge in a thrilling European Cup Winners' Cup semi-final second leg in Italy.

24 April 1999

A brilliant individual goal from Nwankwo Kanu puts Arsenal 5-0 up away to Middlesbrough with just an hour played. It's the second goal in as many minutes and the pick of the bunch so far, as Lee Dixon's low cross into the box finds Kanu, who allows the ball to move past his front foot before flicking it with the inside of his right boot and directing the ball into the bottom-left corner with Mark Schwarzer having no chance of saving it. Brilliant from the mercurial Nigerian!

24 August 2003

Sol Campbell's superb through pass opens up the Middlesbrough defence as the Gunners take a decisive 4-0 lead at the Riverside Stadium. The England defender spots the run of Freddie Ljungberg on the right and plays a ball into his path, and the Swedish forward drives into the box before unselfishly squaring for Sylvain Wiltord to bundle home his second of the afternoon.

6 December 2003

A superb break down the left flank opens up Leicester City's defence and ends with Arsenal taking a 1-0 lead. Robert Pires, deep inside his own half, plays a fine ball with the outside of his right foot to Dennis Bergkamp, who feigns a movement that fools his marker and allows him to run clear – he looks up, crosses into the middle and Gilberto Silva does the rest, powering a header home from six yards out.

13 November 2004

Patrick Vieira puts the Gunners 3-1 up at White Hart Lane – the third Arsenal goal in 15 minutes. The French midfielder wins possession just inside the Spurs half before brushing off a challenge and finishing emphatically from inside the box with a drive that gives Paul Robinson no chance.

9 January 2007

Júlio Baptista, having just missed a penalty, scores a superb long-range effort to make it 5-1 for Arsenal at Anfield in the League Cup quarter-final. It is the excellent Jérémie Aliadière who makes the opportunity, skipping past a challenge on the left before playing a precision pass to Baptista, who drills a low shot past Jerzy Dudek from 22 yards out to complete a well-deserved hat-trick.

7 November 2012

Santi Cazorla gets the goal his display deserves as Arsenal go 4-1 up against Tottenham. Theo Walcott and Lukas Podolski combine down the left and the German striker's low cross is drilled home by Santi Cazorla to put the Gunners out of sight with 30 minutes still to play.

10 August 2014

With just an hour of the 2014 FA Community Shield played, Arsenal increase their advantage over Manchester City to 3-0. Olivier Giroud receives the ball 25 yards from goal and holds off a challenge from behind, before teeing himself up and striking a shot that takes a slight deflection from Matija Nastasić before ending up in the roof of the City net to effectively end the contest.

23 November 2016

Arsenal go 2-1 up against PSG at the Emirates. The goal has more than a shade of good fortune about it as Carl Jenkinson's cross from the right just evades Aaron Ramsey, but as an attempt is made to clear the ball it strikes Marco Verratti on the shins and pings past his own keeper to give the Gunners the lead for the first time in either of the Champions League group stage clashes.

24 January 2018

Granit Xhaka scores what proves to be the decisive goal of the Carabao Cup second-leg tie with Chelsea. Xhaka finds Alexandre Lacazette on the right of the box and his attempted cross deflects into the path of Xhaka, who prods the ball home from close range to make it 2-1 on the night and on aggregate – enough to send the Gunners to Wembley, where Manchester City will be the opposition.

9 December 2019

Gabriel Martinelli levels for Arsenal against West Ham United at The London Stadium. Trailing through a first-half header from Ogbonna, Sead Kolašinac attacks down the left before playing a precision low ball into the box, where Martinelli expertly diverts it into the bottom right of the net to start a spell of dominance that will see the Gunners score three times in quick succession.

61

23 December 1978

A decisive moment at White Hart Lane as Arsenal go 3-0 up against Spurs. The sublime Liam Brady is again the creator-in-chief as the Republic of Ireland midfielder collects the ball on the left before gliding towards the Spurs box, tormenting three defenders, before sending the perfect cross towards the far post for compatriot Frank Stapleton to meet it with a diving header and seemingly put the game beyond the hosts.

22 October 2005

Arsenal finally break down a stubborn Manchester City at Highbury with the opening goal of the game. Kolo Touré sends a pass through to Thierry Henry who uses his pace to just nip in ahead of goalkeeper David James, who makes contact and the referee points to the spot. Robert Pires – who has missed his previous spot kick at Highbury – steps up to confidently despatch a rising shot past James to make it 1-0 – but the second penalty of the game 11 minutes later is anything but as clinical ...

9 March 2015

Danny Welbeck scores what will prove to be the goal that sends Arsenal into the FA Cup semi-finals. The former Manchester United striker chases a poor back pass by Antonio Valencia and just gets to the ball before David de Gea, tapping it past the Spanish goalkeeper on the edge of the box before beating two defenders to the ball and rolling a shot into the unguarded net as the Gunners record a thrilling victory at Old Trafford.

62

16 April 1980

Alan Sunderland equalises for Arsenal in the FA Cup semi-final replay at Villa Park. The Gunners have fallen behind 11 minutes earlier when David Fairclough gives Liverpool the lead, but a calculated defensive risk allows Arsenal to draw level. David Price lofts a pass over the Liverpool defence for Sunderland to race on to – but though the Merseysiders stand with their arms raised waiting for the offside flag, the officials wave play on and Sunderland coolly chips the ball over Ray Clemence and celebrates a superb goal even before the ball crosses the line.

11 September 2004

Having survived one or two close calls, Arsenal finally edge ahead against Fulham at Craven Cottage. The move starts with José Antonio Reyes who spots Ashley Cole in space on the left flank – he plays a low pass into the path of Reyes who is now on the edge of the box and he moves it on to Thierry Henry, who drags the ball back a fraction and shifts his feet before poking it into space for Freddie Ljungberg to run on to and drill a low shot home.

6 November 2013

Arsenal become the first English side to win at the Westfalenstadion as Arsène Wenger's side claim an impressive and vital victory over Borussia Dortmund in the Champions League group stage clash in Germany.

After soaking up intense pressure against the Bundesliga side, the breakthrough – and only goal of the game – comes when Mesut Özil's cross is nodded on by Olivier Giroud and Aaron Ramsey heads home from close range to make it 1-0 and boost hopes of progressing from Group F, where Dortmund and Napoli are also battling to qualify for the knockout stages. It is the Gunners' first attempt on target.

30 May 2015

Arsenal all but seal victory against Aston Villa in the 2015 FA Cup Final. Leading 2-0 thanks to fine goals from Theo Walcott and Alexis Sánchez, the third of the game is simplicity itself as a corner from the right finds the head of the unmarked Per Mertesacker, who makes no mistake from the edge of the six-yard box to put the Gunners three goals to the good and totally in command of the game.

63

6 December 1930

Arsenal's game against Grimsby Town is abandoned due to poor visibility. The First Division clash ends as thick fog descends on Highbury and the match has to be rescheduled for the following month – a game which the Gunners go on to win 9-1.

20 April 1950

Arsenal, leading 1-0 against Liverpool in the 1950 FA Cup Final, double their lead with a superb second of the game from Reg Lewis. A sublime flick from Freddie Cox releases Lewis inside the box and the Gunners' no. 10 lashes a low right-foot shot past Cyril Sidlow to make it 2-0 to Tom Whittaker's side. The Wembley brace is fitting reward for Lewis who spends his entire 18-year career at Highbury, bagging 116 goals in 176 matches but losing perhaps his best years to the Second World War.

4 May 2003

Having fallen behind again to relegation-threatened Leeds United, Arsenal pull the score back to 2-2 in a tense match at Highbury. Anything other than a win will all but hand the Premier League title to Manchester United so the equaliser reinvigorates the Gunners fans who start to believe again. The goal is typical of this thrilling Arsène Wenger side as Thierry Henry feeds Robert Pires on the left of the box and the French winger dashes to the line before playing a pass into the six-yard box, where Dennis Bergkamp arrives first to flick the ball home from close range. Leeds go on to grab a late winner – just as they had done in 1999 – to hand the title to their fiercest rivals Manchester United (just as they had done in 1999). This will be the last game Arsenal lose before embarking on the 49-game 'Invincibles' run.

7 February 2004

The Gunners earn breathing space with a third goal against Wolves at Molineux. After a Thierry Henry corner is cleared out as far as Gilberto Silva, he plays it to Robert Pires, who whips in a deep cross to the far post – Patrick Vieira nods it back into the six-yard box and Kolo Touré heads past the keeper for a rare goal and a 3-1 lead. It is enough to seal victory and beat a club record 24th unbeaten game set by George Graham's side in 1990/91.

26 December 2019

New head coach Mikel Arteta's tenure begins with a trip to Bournemouth on Boxing Day. The former Gunners midfielder and Manchester City coach watches from the dugout as his side come from 1-0 down to the Cherries at the Vitality Stadium to claim a 1-1 draw courtesy of Pierre-Emerick Aubameyang, who drills home after Reiss Nelson's shot from the edge of the box is pushed out.

64

29 October 2009

Emmanuel Adebayor taps home from close range as Arsenal go 3-1 up against Tottenham at an electric Emirates Stadium. Samir Nasri gets to the ball first in the box and chips it over keeper Heurelho Gomes, but with a defender chasing the ball towards the net, Adebayor makes sure by ensuring the goal is scored as the Gunners seemingly head towards three points ... only there will be a dramatic twist later in the game.

30 October 2012

Arsenal pull another goal back to make one or two Reading fans a little twitchy. The home side have raced into a 4-0 lead but when Olivier Giroud sends a bullet header past Adam Federici from a Theo Walcott corner, the Gunners have halved the hosts' lead with plenty of time remaining in the Capital One Cup fourth-round clash in Berkshire.

29 December 2012

In a seesaw encounter, Arsenal take the lead for a third time against Newcastle United at the Emirates. Lukas Podolski feeds Jack Wilshere just outside the Magpies box and the Gunners' playmaker weaves past a couple of challenges and delays just long enough to send a delicate chip into the box where it is headed off the line – but only as far as Podolski, who has the simplest of tasks to nod home from two yards out.

65

12 October 1953

Roared on by a Highbury crowd of almost 40,000, the Gunners take a 2-1 lead over Blackpool in the FA Charity Shield. Jimmy Logie's pass is collected by Cliff Holton – creator of the equaliser – and his shot is parried by the keeper and turned home by Doug Lishman to put the hosts ahead for the first time.

8 April 1978

If the first two Malcolm Macdonald goals of the FA Cup semi-final against Orient have been fortuitous, there is nothing lucky about Arsenal's third at Stamford Bridge. Graham Rix sets off from his own half, gliding past two challenges before sending in an angled low, left-foot shot that squirms under the keeper to make it 3-0 and effectively book a place in the final against Bobby Robson's Ipswich Town.

23 December 1978

One of the best Arsenal goals of all time? If not the best, certainly one of the best and one of the most famous. Fortunately, the *Match of the Day* cameras are present at White Hart Lane as Liam Brady scores a brilliant individual goal to put the Gunners 4-0 up. Brady wins possession on the edge of the box and moves in a yard before bending a left-foot shot into the top-right corner that any Brazilian would have been proud of. In fact, the momentum from much of the slice he puts on the shot sees Brady almost spin around and memorably, BBC commentator John Motson says, 'Look at that! Oh look at that! What a goal by Brady!' The goal is later voted as the *Match of the Day* Goal of the Season for 1978/79. Deservedly so.

22 August 2004

Robert Pires arrives at the back post to tap home the goal that makes it 3-3 with Middlesbrough at Highbury. The Gunners have been trailing by two goals but Thierry Henry receives the ball on the edge of the box after a terrific run by Cesc Fàbregas, beats his man but is pushed out wide and he manages to put a low ball across the six-yard box for Pires to level the scores and send Highbury wild.

22 August 2004

Less than a minute after levelling the scores against Middlesbrough, José Antonio Reyes sends Highbury ballistic with a superb goal to put the Gunners 4-3 up. Dennis Bergkamp drives through the middle of the park, nutmegging one Boro player before threading the ball to Reyes, who cuts inside of one challenge before firing a howitzer of a shot into the top right-hand corner.

11 September 2004

After keeping Arsenal at bay for more than an hour, Fulham concede a second goal in three minutes as an intricate move ends with Zat Knight challenging Freddie Ljungberg as Dennis Bergkamp's pass comes into the box, but it is the Fulham defender who gets the final touch, poking it past his own keeper to double the Gunners' lead at Craven Cottage.

24 January 2006

Kerrea Gilbert, making a rare start at right-back for the Gunners, plays a key role in Arsenal levelling the League Cup semi-final second leg aggregate at Highbury. Trailing to a 1-0 first leg loss to the Latics, Gilbert bursts on an overlapping run, receives the ball and then crosses for Thierry Henry to head home from five yards out and make it 1-0 on the night and 1-1 overall.

15 September 2007

Arsenal level the scores at White Hart Lane with a fairly straightforward set piece against Spurs. The hosts have led through a first-half Gareth Bale free kick and the Gunners respond in kind as Cesc Fàbregas whips in a free kick from the left flank and Emmanuel Adebayor beats the keeper to the ball and nods home the equaliser.

26 February 2012

The foundations of the Emirates are rocking as the Gunners go 4-2 up against Tottenham. A counter-attack sees the ball work its way to Robin van Persie who holds the ball up long enough for Theo Walcott to race down the middle, receive the Dutch striker's pass and deftly lift the ball over Brad Friedel.

29 December 2013

Arsenal return to St James' Park to defeat Newcastle United 1-0 with a second-half winner set up by Theo Walcott – just as the Gunners had done the previous May when Champions League football had been secured. That goal had also been the result of a free kick and this one is also, as Walcott dinks a central set piece into the box for Olivier Giroud to gracefully guide past the keeper with a clever header. It is three points that ensure Arsenal go into 2014 as Premier League leaders.

66

2 May 1992

Arsenal take on Southampton in front of what will be the last day for the North Bank terrace. Gunners fans have stood on the famous old steps since 1913, so there is plenty of nostalgia and emotion in the air as the teams come out for what is also the last First Division game before it becomes the rebranded Premier League. A crowd of 37,702 are inside Highbury with thousands crammed on the North Bank for one last time. The game is in danger of becoming something of an anticlimax with no goals after more than an hour of action, but finally, Kevin Campbell breaks the deadlock as Paul Merson's corner is nodded into the six-yard box and Campbell makes just enough connection to send the ball over the keeper and put Arsenal 1-0 up.

15 May 2004

How fitting it is that skipper Patrick Vieira scores the goal that not only wins the game against Leicester City, but also ensures the Gunners become 'The Invincibles', as they complete the 38-game Premier League campaign without losing a single match. Vieira plays a short pass to Dennis Bergkamp in midfield before suddenly bursting forward into the box – of course, Bergkamp's pass is inch-perfect and Vieira arrives with perfect timing to nick the ball away from the keeper and roll the ball home to send Highbury wild. It is the first time a side has remained unbeaten in a league campaign since Preston North End in 1888/89 and a remarkable feat by a quite magnificent group of players who are also 40 matches unbeaten in league football overall. The Gunners, at this point, are still two games away from Nottingham Forest's 42-match unbeaten run ...

18 September 2004

Freddie Ljungberg's first touch from a crossfield pass sees him accelerate away from his marker and his low cross into the box is cleverly back-flicked into the net by Robert Pires to put the Gunners 2-1 up at Highbury against Bolton Wanderers. Though the visitors level again shortly after, the 2-2 draw extends Arsenal's unbeaten league run to an incredible 46 games.

24 October 2010

Alex Song curls a delightful shot into the top corner of the net to give Joe Hart no chance as Arsenal take a 2-0 lead against ten-man Manchester City. The goal just about ends City's hopes of a comeback and helps the Gunners towards three crucial points at a frustrated Etihad.

9 December 2019

A sumptuous strike from Nicolas Pépé puts Arsenal 2-1 up against West Ham United at The London Stadium. Pierre-Emerick Aubameyang probes forward before playing a short pass to Pépé, who quickly shifts inside of his marker before curling a powerful left-foot shot into the top-left corner for only his second Gunners goal to that point – but what a strike.

67

1 August 1999

Nwankwo Kanu scores from the spot to make it 1-1 in the 1999 FA Charity Shield clash with Manchester United at Wembley. Patrick Vieira, who has earlier had a penalty appeal turned down, has his shirt tugged by United full-back Dennis Irwin in the box and the referee awards a penalty. Kanu sends keeper Mark Bosnich the wrong way.

26 September 2003

Gilberto Silva powers home a header from close range as Arsenal regain the lead against Newcastle United. On a night of incessant rain in North London, Robert Pires sends a free kick in from the right and Gilberto leaps to head past the keeper from eight yards out to make it 2-1 and claim his first Highbury goal.

16 April 2004

Thierry Henry continues to drive Arsenal towards the Premier League title with yet another stunning effort – his fourth of the night – against Leeds United. The Frenchman has become almost unplayable, such is his devastating brilliance and sky-high confidence and pace. Robert Pires receives the ball on the halfway line and touches it to his left, where Henry races between two Leeds players and then turns on the afterburners to speed between two more defenders before hitting a low shot past the keeper to make it 5-0. It is his 150th goal for the club and he becomes the first Arsenal player since Ian Wright in December 1991 to score four goals in one game. From one Arsenal legend to another!

21 April 2009

Andrey Arshavin scores his second of the night away to Liverpool with a superb strike. The Russian collects a sloppy pass from Arbeloa and only has one thought in his mind, as he drives towards the edge of the box before unleashing a swerving howitzer of a shot that gives Pepe Reina no chance and makes it 2-2 on the night.

68

18 April 1993

Arsenal come from behind to take what proves to be a decisive 2-1 lead against Sheffield Wednesday in the 1993 League Cup Final. Paul Merson is the architect as he skips past former Gunner Viv Anderson on the left flank before his low cross is only half cleared as far as Steve Morrow, who drills home from close range to put his team on the way to only a second-ever League Cup win. The teams will meet again a month later in the FA Cup Final, with Arsenal again edging a tight game. During the after-match celebrations, match-winner Morrow falls off Tony Adams's shoulders and breaks his arm, ruling him out of the FA Cup Final!

26 September 2003

A goal worthy of winning any game. Liverpool fail to clear the danger on the edge of their own box and the ball eventually lands at the feet of Robert Pires, who only has one thing in mind as he shifts slightly to the right before curling a 25-yard howitzer into the far top right of the Liverpool net. The Gunners hold out to secure a vital 2-1 victory and remain unbeaten – and top of the Premier League going into the international break.

10 January 2004

Arsenal get the fourth goal needed to send them back to the top of the Premier League table ahead of Manchester

United. Nwankwo Kanu plays a big part in the move that leads to the goal, wriggling past a couple of challenges before passing to his right where Freddie Ljungberg hits a crisp low drive that hits the far post and rolls into the opposite corner of the Boro net – but a late penalty for the visitors denies top spot in the table despite the 4-1 victory over Steve McLaren's side.

14 January 2006

Thierry Henry equals Cliff Bastin's record of 150 league goals with a typically precise finish. The elegant French striker races clear of a pedestrian Middlesbrough defence before drilling a low shot across Brad Jones and into the bottom-left corner to achieve yet another memorable milestone for the Gunners, as well as put his team 6-0 up.

29 October 2009

Robin van Persie restores Arsenal's two-goal advantage as he emphatically thumps home from 12 yards out against Tottenham. Spurs have scored 60 seconds earlier but fine work by Emmanuel Adebayor gives the Dutch striker a great chance and he makes no mistake to put the Gunners 4-2 up in a thrilling North London derby – though Spurs will bag two late goals to secure a 4-4 draw.

26 February 2012

Tottenham can't live with Theo Walcott's electric pace as the forward again breaks the visitors' offside trap. Alex Song's clever pass in behind the Spurs defence leaves Walcott a clear angled run towards goal and his low shot beats the keeper and nestles in the bottom-left corner of the net to make it 5-2, seal three points and complete a blistering spell of five goals in 28 minutes for Arsène Wenger's side.

69

6 April 1995

Paul Merson's superb through ball sees Ian Wright latch on to the pass and turn it past the keeper from the edge of the box. The goal restores the Gunners' two-goal advantage over Sampdoria at Highbury in the European Cup Winners' Cup semi-final first leg – though the Italians will score again to end the tie with a 3-2 win for Stewart Houston's side.

16 May 1998

Arsenal double their lead in the 1998 FA Cup Final as Arsène Wenger's side power their way to a league and FA Cup double. Having gone ahead midway through the first half, the Gunners make it 2-0 against Newcastle United with a goal midway through the second period. Ray Parlour's pass finds Nicolas Anelka – who initially looks offside – and the 19-year-old races clear to drill a low right-foot shot past Shay Given to complete the scoring on a memorable day for the Arsenal supporters. Thankfully, there was no VAR back then!

14 April 1999

FA Cup holders Arsenal fight back to level the scores against Manchester United in the FA Cup semi-final replay at Villa Park. Trailing to a superb first-half strike from David Beckham, the Gunners finally equalise when Dennis Bergkamp's long-range effort deflects off Jaap

Stam to leave Peter Schmeichel no chance and make the score 1-1.

11 August 2002

Gilberto Silva marks his Arsenal debut with the goal that settles the 2002 Community Shield at Wembley against Liverpool. The Brazilian has come on at the start of the second half and when Ashley Cole and Dennis Bergkamp combine, it is the Dutchman's cross that Gilberto squeezes through Jerzy Dudek's legs for the only goal of the game.

8 November 2003

Trailing 1-0 to an early Tottenham goal at Highbury, the Gunners finally level the scores. Ray Parlour's clever pass from his own half sets Thierry Henry free and he races into the box but sees his low shot palmed away by Kasey Keller – but only into the path of Robert Pires, who sweeps home the loose ball from close range to send the Arsenal fans wild and set up a grandstand finish ...

2 October 2004

Arsenal go 3-0 up in the pouring rain at Highbury. This goal is all about José Antonio Reyes and Thierry Henry, who pass between each other on the edge of the box a couple of times before Reyes tees Henry up to fire a swerving bullet of a shot that scrapes the underside of the bar on its way in from 15 yards out.

13 November 2004

Arsenal take a 4-2 lead against Spurs in a rip-roaring North London derby at White Hart Lane. The architect is Cesc

172

Fàbregas who receives the ball on the edge of the Spurs box before playing a glorious reverse pass to Freddie Ljungberg, who drills a low drive past Paul Robinson to put the Gunners back in the driving seat.

9 December 2019

Pierre-Emerick Aubameyang scores Arsenal's third goal in nine minutes to knock the stuffing out of West Ham United at The London Stadium. The Gabon striker has already assisted one goal and his 13th of the season seals a first victory under Freddie Ljungberg's caretaker reign. Aubameyang receives the ball on the edge of the box before playing a back-heel to Nicolas Pépé on the left of the box. As Aubameyang dashes towards the six-yard box, Pépé nonchalantly dinks a cross in his direction and the Arsenal striker makes no mistake with a volley from close range to make it 3-1.

70

21 December 1991

Ian Wright and Anders Limpar complete an extraordinary afternoon at Highbury as Wright bags his fourth goal against Everton and Limpar claims his fourth assist. The fourth goal, more than perhaps the previous three, is down to Limpar's excellence as he chases a wide ball on the right and then skips past a challenge before sending a cross into the six-yard box that Wright can't miss. An exceptional performance by the Swedish winger as the Gunners seal a 4-2 win over the Toffees.

2 May 1992

A third goal in four minutes as Arsenal have taken the lead on 66 minutes only to allow Southampton to level just two minutes later. Just another couple of minutes have lapsed when the Gunners go 2-1 up thanks to an Ian Wright penalty. Paul Merson is brought down in the box by Francis Benali and though Lee Dixon would normally step up, he gives the opportunity to team-mate Ian Wright who is chasing the coveted Golden Boot. Wright has started the day a goal behind Tottenham's Gary Lineker who has added another to his tally that day – but Wright tucks the spot kick away to keep his hopes alive.

4 May 2002

Appearing in their 15th FA Cup Final and second final in succession, the Gunners take on Chelsea at the

Millennium Stadium in Cardiff in an epic London derby. Arsenal have lost the previous year's final and are determined to make amends in this game, but in a tight and evenly contested battle, it isn't until the 70th minute that the Gunners finally break the deadlock – and how. Good work by Sylvain Wiltord finds Ray Parlour and the Arsenal midfielder cuts inside one challenge before curling a beauty into the top right-hand corner of the goal to make it 1-0.

2 October 2004

José Antonio Reyes puts the icing on the cake as the Gunners score a second goal in as many minutes to go 4-0 up against Charlton Athletic. In a lovely, sweeping move across the pitch, Dennis Bergkamp plays the ball to the overlapping Reyes who hits an angled, crisp low shot into the bottom-right corner as Arsenal complete their 48th league game without loss.

11 May 2005

When Thierry Henry flicks the ball up in the Everton box, Lee Carsley instinctively tries to stop it with his upper arm and the referee immediately points to the penalty spot. The Arsenal players present the ball to Edu, playing his last game for the club, and the Brazilian steps up and just squeezes in his first Highbury goal for 18 months and increases the Gunners' lead to 5-0.

21 April 2009

Andrey Arshavin completes his hat-trick to put Arsenal 3-2 up at Anfield in a thrilling Premier League game. Having just levelled three minutes earlier, Arshavin profits from a poor clearance as Samir Nasri's cross comes into the box and he makes no mistake from close range to send the travelling Gunners fans wild.

14 February 2016

Arsenal finally equalise against Premier League leaders Leicester City at the Emirates. Trailing to Jamie Vardy's first-half penalty, Olivier Giroud superbly cushions a header down as Héctor Bellerín's cross comes into the box for Theo Walcott, who makes no mistake with a precise finish from close in.

30 October 2019

Having seen a 4-2 lead wiped out in the space of four second-half minutes at Anfield, Joe Willock restores Arsenal's lead over Liverpool as this thrilling Carabao Cup tie takes yet another twist. Willock shoots from 20 yards out into the top left-hand corner to make it 5-4 for the Gunners in this breathless encounter, but the hosts will go on to level in added time to make it 5-5 on the night and then go on to win the penalty shoot-out 5-4. It is the first time an away team scores five goals at Anfield and still ends up losing!

71

11 September 2004

José Antonio Reyes – a second-half sub – scores Arsenal's third goal to complete a 3-0 win at Fulham. Reyes, who has been involved in the first two goals, is put clear by a deft Dennis Bergkamp pass before firing an angled shot into the right corner of the Cottagers net and, in doing so, ensuring the unbeaten league run is extended to 45 matches.

17 May 2014

Trailing 2-1 with 19 minutes of normal time remaining of the 2014 FA Cup Final, Arsenal get a huge slice of luck when a corner is awarded despite the last touch being from Yaya Sanogo. From the resulting corner, Bacary Sagna's deflected header lands in the six-yard box and Laurent Koscielny manages to get the merest of touches to help it past Hull City goalkeeper Allan McGregor to make it 2-2 and send the Gunners fans wild at Wembley.

23 April 2017

Trailing 1-0 to Manchester City in the FA Cup semi-final at Wembley, Arsenal get back on level terms with a superb equaliser. Alex Oxlade-Chamberlain receives the ball on the right flank and whips a deep cross into the six-yard box, where Nacho Monreal arrives with immaculate timing to volley the ball past Claudio Bravo from close range and make the score 1-1 against Pep Guardiola's side.

72

9 August 1998

A superb pass from Patrick Viera sends Nicolas Anelka clear to complete a 3-0 FA Charity Shield win over Manchester United at Wembley. The French midfielder plays a pass with the outside of his boot from the halfway line into Anelka's path and the young striker does the rest, outpacing a labouring Jaap Stam before tucking the ball past Peter Schmeichel's near post to end the game as a contest and secure a ninth Charity Shield success for Arsenal.

8 April 2001

Despite being denied by several fine saves by Tottenham keeper Neil Sullivan, the Gunners finally get the goal that secures a place in the FA Cup Final. Scorer of the equaliser in the semi-final at Old Trafford, the imperious Patrick Vieira powers forward, winning a challenge and then beating a couple more Spurs players in his driving run before laying the ball off to Sylvain Wiltord on the right flank, and his low cross is turned home by Robert Pires at the far post to put Arsenal 2-1 up against their North London rivals.

11 May 2002

Arsenal regain the lead with a second goal of the game from Thierry Henry. The move starts with Richard Wright throwing the ball to Edu, who progresses to the halfway line and then chips a 30-yard pass into Henry's path, and the Gunners' top scorer hits a clever low shot past the keeper to make it 3-2 and rack up his 23rd league goal of the season in the process.

31 August 2003

Manchester City's defence have only themselves to blame as Freddie Ljungberg puts Arsenal 2-1 up at the City of Manchester Stadium (in its pre-Etihad sponsored days). A succession of poor passes and decisions by the Blues leads to Ljungberg winning possession and finding Sylvain Wiltord, whose flick towards Robert Pires seems to be heading towards David Seaman – but Jihai Sun's attempt to shield allows Pires to force a mistake from Seaman and Ljungberg follows up to prod the loose ball into the net and secure three hard-earned points.

16 October 2004

The Gunners wrap up game 49 of an unbeaten run that stretches back some 19 months with a second Robert Pires goal of the afternoon. As ever, it's a thing of beauty as Thierry Henry casually nudges on a low cross into the box for the unmarked Pires to fire a low drive home and complete a 3-1 win over Aston Villa. Some 36 wins, 13 draws and 112 goals scored, the run will finally end in the next match away to Manchester United.

22 October 2005

Some things look better on the training pitch than they do in real matches and the penalty Arsenal attempt against Manchester City is a case in point. The Gunners, who have gone ahead through a Robert Pires penalty 11 minutes earlier, are awarded a second spot kick by referee Mike Riley after Stephen Jordan fouls Dennis Bergkamp in the box. What follows next is a major embarrassment to Pires and Thierry Henry and clearly angers City players. After plotting to repeat a penalty Johan Cruyff had once done where he runs up but only taps the ball into the path of team-mate Jesper Olsen who plays the ball back to Cruyff who then scores, Pires runs up and wafts his foot over the ball, trying to roll it to his left with his studs – but the contact is minimal, the ball doesn't roll and Henry is left in front of goal but the ball is still behind him – City defender Sylvain Distin runs up and clears the ball before the referee awards City a free kick. Though the Gunners haven't broken any rules, the incident causes a huge debate about whether the attempt is in the spirit of the game. Come what may, the Gunners win 1-0 and haven't attempted that penalty routine since!

73

29 December 2012

In a thrilling Emirates clash, Arsenal go ahead for the fourth time against Newcastle United who have responded to each of the Gunners' three previous goals with an equaliser. Kieran Gibbs sends a low cross towards the penalty spot and Theo Walcott stops the ball before despatching a right-foot shot into the top left-hand corner to make it 4-3.

74

25 April 1936

Almost six years to the day since Arsenal first won the FA Cup, the Gunners are able to celebrate a second success in the competition. Taking on Second Division Sheffield United in front of more than 93,000 fans at Wembley, the Gunners largely dominate proceedings and start as strong favourites to land the coveted trophy. The Blades, however, resist everything that is thrown at them – until the 74th minute with a goal that involves two of the men who had created the opening goal in the 1930 FA Cup Final. Cliff Bastin dribbles past Blades captain Harry Hooper before whipping a cross into the box, where Ted Drake is on hand to drive a left-footed shot into the roof of the net for what proves to be the only goal of the game.

18 October 2005

An historic moment for Thierry Henry, who moves ahead of Ian Wright to become Arsenal's record goalscorer. Henry, who has equalled the record with a goal earlier in the game, collects a long pass from Pires and holds off two defenders on the edge of the box before slotting the ball home to secure a 2-0 victory and, more importantly, confirm his position as the Gunners' record goalscorer with his 186th strike in 303 appearances. A remarkable achievement from a quite sublime footballer.

2 December 2018

Second-half sub Aaron Ramsey is again integral as he wins possession on the halfway line before playing a pass across the pitch to Alexandre Lacazette. The French striker controls and then, with the Tottenham defenders backing off, he hits a low shot – losing his balance as he does so – that tucks inside the left post and out of Hugo Lloris's reach to make it 3-2.

75

28 April 1970

John Radford heads Arsenal level on aggregate in the Inter-Cities Fairs Cup Final second leg at Highbury. The Gunners, needing two goals to level the scores having lost the first leg 3-1, double their lead as Bob McNab's deep cross from the left finds Radford who nods down and into the left-hand corner to send the North Bank wild and make it 3-3 overall.

23 October 1999

Nwankwo Kanu starts a remarkable comeback for Arsenal at Stamford Bridge with what will be his first of three goals in 15 unforgettable minutes. With Chelsea leading 2-0 and looking comfortable, when Marc Overmars's shot is blocked, Kanu is first to react, prodding home a low drive past Ed de Goey to give the Gunners hope.

28 October 2000

Arsenal make the points safe at Highbury with a third goal against Manchester City, who have been reduced to ten men since the 43rd minute. The goal comes as a result of a slick counter-attack that sees Dennis Bergkamp find Thierry Henry midway inside the City half, and the French genius slips a threaded pass into the path of Sylvain Wiltord who makes no mistake with a low shot from the edge of the box that seems to go through keeper Nicky Weaver's legs.

28 September 1991

Alan Smith and Anders Limpar combine to allow Ian Wright to complete a dream league debut away to Southampton. The Gunners' £2.5 million signing from Crystal Palace has scored in the League Cup in midweek but marks an incredible First Division debut with a hat-trick, as Limpar finds Smith in the Saints box and the England striker sees his low shot parried by the keeper, but Wright uses his electric pace to get to the loose ball before anyone else and make it 4-0. Wright will finish the season with 31 goals and, in the last game of the 1991/92 campaign, score another hat-trick against Southampton. It will be his third treble of an unforgettable first season at Highbury.

18 October 2003

Just moments after making a superb save, Carlo Cudicini gifts Thierry Henry the winning goal in a tough London derby with Chelsea. Robert Pires sends in a low cross from the right but it looks like an easy claim for Cudicini, but as he goes down to grab the ball, he takes his eye off it for a split second and it rolls beneath his body and into the path of Henry, who taps into the empty net to give Arsenal a 2-1 victory.

4 October 2009

A lovely, free-flowing and lightning-fast break down the left flank sees Gaël Clichy play a low ball into the box where the irrepressible Cesc Fàbregas deftly touches the pass on to Theo Walcott, who drills a low shot past Blackburn Rovers keeper Paul Robinson to put the Gunners 5-2 ahead at the Emirates.

76

28 April 1970

John Sammels sends Highbury crazy with a superbly taken third goal in the Inter-Cities Fairs Cup Final. Having just gone 2-0 up and levelled the aggregate score at 3-3, Charlie George immediately launches another attack on the Anderlecht goal, cutting in from the left before launching a long ball towards Sammels, who controls it on his chest before racing into the box and drilling a low shot past the keeper to make it 4-3 overall and 3-0 on the night to seal Arsenal's first European triumph.

19 April 1972

John Radford completes the Gunners' comeback as he scores what proves to be the winning goal in the FA Cup semi-final replay against Stoke City at Goodison Park. Having gone behind in the first half to a Jimmy Greenhoff penalty, Arsenal also level from the spot in the second half and the scorer, Charlie George, sets up the winner as well – but in highly controversial circumstances. The live-wire forward receives the ball from Peter Storey but is a good couple of yards offside – legend has it the linesman mistakes a programme seller by the edge of the pitch for a Stoke defender and waves play on – George then sends in a measured low cross that Radford sweeps home from close range to make it 2-1. George's unusual celebration is almost as memorable as the goal! Stoke, understandably, are distraught as they are again denied a place in the cup final.

7 May 2006

Thierry Henry ensures Arsenal's final game at Highbury is marked with a victory as he completes a hat-trick against Paul Jewell's Wigan Athletic. Henry bags his 137th Highbury goal from the penalty spot after Andreas Johansson has pulled back Freddie Ljungberg in the box resulting in a red card for the Latics player. Henry steps up to send the goalkeeper the wrong way and complete a 4-2 victory in the last game at Highbury. After scoring, Henry kneels down to kiss the turf as news filters through that Tottenham, whose result the Gunners need to better to secure the final Champions League spot, are behind away to West Ham. What a day to be a Gooner!

22 December 2007

Nicklas Bendtner scores the fastest goal by a substitute in Premier League history just 11 seconds after coming on in the North London derby with Tottenham at the Emirates. Drawing 1-1 as the Dane comes off the bench, Bendtner soars to head home a corner with what proves to be the winning goal in a 2-1 win for the Gunners.

77

10 May 1995

John Hartson prods home from close range to bring Arsenal level in the 1995 European Cup Winners' Cup Final. The Welsh striker sweeps home a poked pass from Paul Merson to hit a low shot into the bottom-left corner to make it 1-1 against Real Zaragoza, who go on to win the game in extra time with former Spurs player Nayim's speculative 50-yard lob catching David Seaman by surprise just seconds from the end.

11 May 2005

Dennis Bergkamp gets Arsenal's sixth of the game as he wins the ball midway inside the Everton half and as it loops up high, he brings it down inside the box on his thigh – a little more to the left than he intends – before drilling a low shot past Everton keeper Richard Wright and makes the scoreline 6-0 in front of an ecstatic Highbury.

20 October 2015

Arsenal break the deadlock against Bayern Munich in a must-win Champions League group stage match. The Gunners finally go 1-0 up when Santi Cazorla's dangerous free kick is missed by Manuel Neuer, who misjudges the trajectory completely, and Olivier Giroud bravely dives in to head home from close range.

2 December 2018

Lucas Torreira scores his first Arsenal goal and what a time to do it. The Uruguayan runs on to a sublime reverse pass from Pierre-Emerick Aubameyang before drilling a low shot past Hugo Lloris to make it two goals in less than four minutes, put the Gunners 4-2 up in the North London derby and seal three welcome points.

78

6 September 1913

Archie Devine ensures Arsenal start life at Highbury with a victory. Having trailed to a 20th-minute goal against Leicester Fosse, the Gunners equalise on half-time before the referee awards a penalty for handball 12 minutes from time. Devine steps up to convert the spot kick and secure a 2-1 win on an historic day for the club at their new home.

24 April 1999

The Gunners declare at six as Arsène Wenger's side run riot at the Riverside. Middlesbrough cannot handle Nwankwo Kanu's trickery or Nicolas Anelka's electric pace and the pair combine to put Arsenal 6-0 ahead on Teesside. Kanu weaves inside before playing a short pass to Anelka, who immediately shifts the ball away from his marker before unleashing a powerful shot from 18 yards that the keeper can do little about. It caps a mesmeric performance from both Kanu and Anelka – the latter having a hand in five of the goals that afternoon.

1 August 1999

Ray Parlour scores what proves to be the winning goal in the 1999 Charity Shield clash with Manchester United. In a fiery encounter, the Gunners – who have previously trailed – complete their comeback as Patrick Vieira's header finds Nwankwo Kanu and the Nigerian controls the ball and heads towards goal before laying it off to his right, where the overlapping Parlour drills home from 15 yards.

11 May 2003

Arsenal go 3-0 up at relegated Sunderland with a goal made by Thierry Henry brilliance. The woeful hosts are the architects of their own downfall yet again as a terrible pass in the Arsenal half is intercepted by Henry, who glides forward and then delightfully flicks a ball between two Sunderland defenders and into the path of Freddie Ljungberg, who dinks the ball over the keeper for his second of the afternoon.

9 April 2004

Thierry Henry completes his hat-trick against Liverpool with the scrappiest of his treble. Dennis Bergkamp lifts a wonderful pass over the Liverpool defence and into the path of Henry who sees his first effort saved by Jerzy Dudek – but the ball bounces back on to the Arsenal striker and into the net to make it 4-2 and seals another three points. It also leaves Arsène Wenger's men seven points clear with seven games remaining and within sight of remaining unbeaten for an entire Premier League campaign ...

16 February 2011

Trailing 1-0 in the Champions League round of 16 first-leg tie against Barcelona, Arsenal equalise to send the Emirates Stadium wild. Robin van Persie runs on to a pass on the left of the Barcelona box and, seeming as though he is about to pull the ball back into the middle, the Dutch striker fires past Victor Valdes from an acute angle to make it 1-1.

13 September 2016

Alexis Sánchez scores a vital equaliser at the Parc des Princes as the Gunners secure a 1-1 draw with Paris Saint-Germain. The home side have been ahead since the first minute with Edinson Cavani scoring after just 44 seconds, but when Mesut Özil finds Alex Iwobi in the box, the Nigerian sees his shot parried out by Alphonse Areola – but only as far as Sánchez, who rifles home the rebound.

7 March 2020

A lengthy VAR review of Alexandre Lacazette's goal against West Ham United sees it eventually awarded. Lacazette sweeps home from close range after Mesut Özil's clever cushioned header but the goal is checked after the suspicion of a marginal offside. The officials take their time before finally confirming the goal is legitimate – and it proves to be enough to see off the Hammers at the Emirates.

One of the most iconic celebrations in FA Cup Final history as Charlie George lies on the Wembley turf having just scored against Liverpool.

Alan Sunderland scores a last-minute winner against Manchester United in the 1979 FA Cup Final at Wembley.

Charlie Nicholas scores against Liverpool in the 1987 Littlewoods Cup Final at Wembley.

Nigel Winterburn celebrates as Michael Thomas scores the last-gasp goal against Liverpool that means Arsenal are champions.

Another masterful goal from the Dutch genius that was Dennis Bergkamp who bags a later leveller away to Leicester to earn a 3-3 draw.

Dennis Bergkamp scores one of the most famous Premier League goals for Arsenal av

Newcastle United

Ian Wright celebrates goal No.179 for Arsenal and finally breaking Cliff Bastin's long-standing record.

Nwankwo Kanu completes a 15-minute hat-trick with a 90th-minute winner from an impossible angle as the Gunners come from 2-0 down to win 3-2 against Chelsea.

Ray Parlour scores with a sumptuous 25-yard shot against Chelsea in the 2002 FA Cup Final.

Sylvain Wiltord marks his 100th Arsenal appearance by scoring the goal that clinches the Double for the Gunners with a 1-0 win over Manchester United at Old Trafford.

Andrei Arshavin celebrates scoring his fourth goal at Anfield in a thrilling match with Liverpool.

Thierry Henry scores against Blackburn Rovers as Arsenal break Nottingham Forest's 42-match unbeaten league record with a 3-0 win at Highbury.

79

8 November 2003

Arsenal grab the winner and settle the North London derby with just 11 minutes remaining. Dennis Bergkamp plays a ball into Nwankwo Kanu in space midway inside the Spurs half. Kanu then finds Freddie Ljungberg on his left and the Swedish forward fires a shot goalwards that strikes the outstretched boot of Stephen Carr, loops up and over Kasey Keller in goal and into the back of the net to make it 2-1 and seal three vital points at an ecstatic Highbury.

8 August 2004

Arsenal go 3-1 up at the Millennium Stadium with a goal made by Ashley Cole. Robin van Persie lobs a short pass into the path of Cole who squeezes the ball past Gary Neville and David Bellion to leave the Gunners' left-back inside the United box, and as he tries to square the ball into the middle, it hits Mikaël Silvestre and rolls past Tim Howard to effectively seal victory for Arsène Wenger's men. Terrific play by Cole as Arsenal secure a 12th Charity Shield/Community Shield success.

25 August 2004

Arsenal's Invincibles achieve immortality as they round off victory over Blackburn Rovers with a third goal of the evening. Thierry Henry races on to a loose pass from a Rovers defender and sprints clear, but his shot is initially well saved – he collects the ball again and waits for the right moment before squaring the ball to the incoming José Antonio Reyes, who makes no mistake from eight yards. It takes Arsenal's unbeaten league run to 43 games and eclipses Brian Clough's Nottingham Forest's 42-match unbeaten run, set some 26 years earlier. Incredible stuff.

27 May 2017

Despite having seen Victor Moses sent off, Premier League champions Chelsea have levelled on 76 minutes of the 2017 FA Cup Final with Diego Costa making it 1-1. But the Gunners strike back quickly when sub Olivier Giroud, only on the pitch for a minute or so, gets to the byline and crosses into the six-yard box where Aaron Ramsey arrives first to head past Thibaut Courtois and make it 2-1 – a lead Arsenal deservedly hold on to and secure a record 13th FA Cup success.

80

12 October 1953

Doug Lishman scores his second goal of the game to seal a 3-1 FA Charity Shield victory over Blackpool. The third goal of the contest at Highbury comes when Don Roper's cross is nodded down by Tommy Lawton, who drills home from close range to give the Gunners their seventh shield success, to the delight of the home supporters.

4 April 1993

Arsenal are facing Tottenham in the FA Cup semi-final at Wembley for the second time in one of the highest profile North London derbies yet. In a tense and tight battle, the match seems to be heading for extra time when Paul Merson's free kick finds the head of Tony Adams and the Gunners skipper thumps a header past Erik Thorstvedt for what proves to be the only goal of the game.

5 April 1997

Dennis Bergkamp completes a Stamford Bridge rout as he puts Arsenal 3-0 up against Chelsea. The graceful Dutchman has already had a huge role in the first two goals but as a long ball is played up towards the halfway line, he immediately realises the two Chelsea defenders going for the ball have misjudged its flight and so sets off in anticipation and is left with a clear run on goal – something he was never going to pass up – and he rounds the keeper some 40 yards from goal before slotting a low shot out of the reach of a despairing defender's attempt to clear in the six-yard box. A masterful finish from the Dutch master!

4 May 2002

Having broken the deadlock in the 2002 FA Cup Final just ten minutes earlier, Arsenal score a killer second to secure their eighth FA Cup success. Freddie Ljungberg picks the ball up on the halfway line before running at a tiring Chelsea defence. He drifts past two players with ease and then outmuscles Chelsea captain John Terry before curling a superb shot past Carlo Cudicini from 18 yards to secure victory.

21 September 2003

Looking good for a valuable point away to Manchester United, Patrick Vieira is shown a second yellow card by the referee and the Gunners are reduced to ten men for the final minutes. With the score 0-0, suddenly, Arsenal's unbeaten start to the 2003/04 campaign is under serious threat at Old Trafford ...

26 September 2003

Future Tottenham midfielder Jermaine Jenas gifts the Gunners the chance to settle an entertaining game against Newcastle United at Highbury. With the scores level at 2-2, Robert Pires sends in a corner from the right flank and as several players go to head the ball, Jenas rises highest and his outstretched arm makes contact, resulting in a penalty. Thierry Henry calmly chips the ball down the middle and into the net to secure a hard-fought 3-2 victory for the still unbeaten Arsenal.

22 November 2003

Birmingham City's search for an equaliser at St Andrew's proves to be their undoing as the Gunners counter-attack and double their lead in the blink of an eye. A cross is cleared to the edge of the box where Kanu finds Thierry Henry midway inside his own half – he plays a simple ball into the path of Dennis Bergkamp who sprints into the Birmingham half with three defenders in his trail – as he approaches the keeper it's not a matter of if, just how he will score and on this occasion, with typical grace, he gently lifts it over Maik Taylor to put Arsenal 2-0 up.

15 September 2007

A stunning goal puts Arsenal 2-1 up at White Hart Lane as the Gunners come from behind to edge towards three points. Tomáš Rosický drifts inside from the left and finds Cesc Fàbregas midway inside the Tottenham half. With no immediate challenge on the Spaniard, he nudges it forward before unleashing a fierce rising shot from fully 30 yards that arrows into the top-left corner to send the travelling Arsenal fans wild.

81

13 September 1997

On an unforgettable day, Ian Wright completes his hat-trick to put the Gunners 4-1 up against Bolton Wanderers. Wright claims the match ball on a day he sets a new scoring record for Arsenal and moves on to 180 goals for the club as a result.

25 November 2003

Thierry Henry, having scored one and made another, puts Arsenal 3-1 up away to Inter Milan with a brilliant individual effort. After picking up the ball just inside his own half, Henry races towards the Inter penalty area before cutting inside, then knocking it past the hapless defender before drilling a low left-foot drive past the goalkeeper and into the bottom-right corner of the net.

13 November 2004

Robert Pires seals victory for Arsenal with the Gunners' fifth of an enthralling North London derby at White Hart Lane. Leading 4-3, a defensive scramble sees the ball fall to Pires who takes a touch before slipping a sublime shot from an acute angle past Paul Robinson to make it 5-3 and seal three points, even though Spurs pull a goal back to go on to lose 5-4.

26 September 2015

Alexis Sánchez completes a superb hat-trick to put Arsenal 4-1 up at the King Power Stadium. The Chilean picks the ball up from a throw-in on the left, easily knocking it past N'Golo Kanté before rifling a 25-yard drive into the bottom-left corner that gives Kasper Schmeichel no chance and sends the home fans heading for the exits.

82

22 April 1970

Ray Kennedy scores a vital goal in the first leg of the Inter-Cities Fairs Cup Final away to Anderlecht. Trailing 3-0 to the Belgian side in what will be the final year of the competition, Kennedy's late goal gives the Gunners something to build upon in the second leg at Highbury. More than 37,000 fans watch the game with the return to be played six days later.

23 December 1978

Alan Sunderland completes an unforgettable hat-trick at White Hart Lane as Arsenal go 5-0 up against Spurs. The goal comes as Pat Jennings hits a long punt into the Tottenham half, Frank Stapleton nods it on and Sunderland controls and takes the ball past two defenders before tucking a left-foot shot into the bottom-right corner in front of the ecstatic travelling Arsenal fans.

28 October 2000

Thierry Henry rubs salt in Manchester City's wounds as he puts Arsenal 4-0 up at Highbury. The Gunners are light years ahead of the struggling Manchester side and this goal demonstrates the struggle ahead for the newly promoted club. Sylvain Wiltord torments City defender Spencer Prior a couple of times before finally driving past him and crossing into the box – his pass finds Henry, who tees himself up and then powers a shot into the top-left corner of the net. All too easy for the Gunners!

11 May 2002

Franny Jeffers seals three hard-earned points against his former club Everton. The Toffees have made life difficult for the newly crowned champions but it is Jeffers's goal that seals victory as Dennis Bergkamp finds Thierry Henry on the left of the box, and his pinpoint cross finds the head of Jeffers who nods home from close range to make it 4-2.

20 March 2003

Ten-man Arsenal restore their two-goal advantage over Chelsea at Stamford Bridge to all but book a place in the FA Cup semi-finals. Having lost Pascal Cygan to a second yellow card some 14 minutes earlier and then seen John Terry halve the Gunners' lead, the third goal is crucial and the timing is perfect. With the hosts attempting to build up a head of steam, Lauren cuts in from the right and across a couple of challenges before firing a low shot inside the right post to put Arsenal 3-1 up and send the travelling fans wild.

12 April 2014

Arsenal leave it late to equalise against Championship side Wigan Athletic in the FA Cup semi-final at Wembley. Trailing from Jordi Gomez's 62nd-minute penalty, Uwe Rösler's side look to be heading for a second successive FA Cup Final having beaten Manchester City in the final the season before (and on their way to relegation). The Gunners start the game as strong favourites as they attempt to end a nine-year wait for a trophy, but it isn't until the 82nd minute that Per Mertesacker levels the scores. A corner from the right finds its way to Kieran Gibbs, who mishits his shot into the turf and Mertesacker manages to nod home at the far post and send the game into extra time.

83

31 March 1979

Playing against his former club, Alan Sunderland ensures Wolverhampton Wanderers won't be going to Wembley as he puts the Gunners 2-0 up at Villa Park. Sunderland, who has spent six years with the Black Country side, scoring 30 goals, wins a 50-50 in midfield after a Frank Stapleton header, spins and nutmegs an approaching Wolves defender before drilling a low shot past the keeper to settle the FA Cup semi-final and book a place at Wembley, and a showpiece clash with Manchester United.

5 April 1987

Arsenal grab a late winner to claim the League Cup for the first time in the club's history. Having earlier trailed 1-0 to Liverpool, Charlie Nicholas bags his second of the game – though there is more than a shade of luck about it. Substitute Perry Groves races down the left flank before intelligently cutting the ball back towards the penalty spot where Nicholas arrives to coolly place a low shot past Bruce Grobbelaar and secure a 2-1 victory. TV replays show Nicholas's shot strikes Ronnie Whelan and completely wrong-foots the Liverpool keeper, who just fails to push the shot out as it trickles into the bottom-left corner.

2 May 1992

Paul Merson has created the opening goal of the game and won a penalty as Arsenal lead Southampton 2-1 at

Highbury – and it is the Gunners' playmaker who lays on the third of the afternoon, as his cross finds the head of Alan Smith who sees his cleverly directed effort hit the underside of the bar and go into the net to all but seal victory.

23 October 1999

Nwankwo Kanu brings Arsenal level with his second goal in eight minutes at Stamford Bridge. Marc Overmars persists on the right flank, trying to get the ball across into the Chelsea box and when he finally does, the ball falls to Kanu whose first touch takes him away from his marker and his second is a low shot past de Goey to make it 2-2.

1 February 2004

A quite breathtaking goal seals three points for the Gunners at home to Manchester City. The visitors – who haven't won at Highbury since 1975 – have stayed in the game, despite falling behind after seven minutes, but Thierry Henry ends the contest as he receives a pass from Robert Pires on the edge of the box, before shifting inside a couple of yards and unleashing a howitzer of a shot that arrows into David James's top-left corner from 20 yards. Power, accuracy and brilliance from the France international.

15 August 2004

Robert Pires taps home Arsenal's fourth at Goodison Park after Thierry Henry's effort cannons back off the underside of the crossbar and falls invitingly at the French winger's feet. It completes an impressive 4-1 win over Everton and stretches the 41-game unbeaten run into a third season.

16 February 2011

Having levelled just five minutes earlier, Arsenal score a second goal to lead 2-1 over Pep Guardiola's Barcelona in the Champions League round of 16 first leg. Samir Nasri chases a ball down the right flank before spotting the run of Andrey Arshavin towards the edge of the box and playing a low pass to the Russian, who hits a curling shot first time that the unsighted Victor Valdes can do nothing about. The Emirates erupts and the Gunners have a precious lead to take back to the Nou Camp.

84

20 September 1998

Freddie Ljungberg marks his Arsenal debut with a goal that seals three points against Manchester United. The Swedish forward has only been on the pitch six minutes when an intricate move ends with Stephen Hughes finding Ljungberg in the box with a deft pass, and he in turn lobs Peter Schmeichel to complete a 3-0 victory at Highbury.

13 April 2003

David Seaman, making his 1,000th senior appearance, produces a superb one-handed save to preserve Arsenal's narrow lead over Sheffield United. Leading 1-0 in the FA Cup semi-final clash at Old Trafford, the Blades look certain to level when sub Paul Peschisolido heads Carl Asaba's shot towards goal from just a couple of yards out, but the 39-year-old Seaman defies his age as he claws the ball clear. It is a save that proves to be the moment that ends the second tier side's hopes.

19 August 2006

Brazilian Gilberto is the first Arsenal player to score in a competitive fixture at the Emirates Stadium. The Gunners look set to lose their first game at their new home with Aston Villa leading 1-0, but teenage sub Theo Walcott's cross into the box finds Gilberto, who thumps a shot into the roof of the net to earn a point and ensure Arsène Wenger's men don't get off on the wrong foot on their new home soil.

14 January 2006

Alexander Hleb scores his first Arsenal goal as the Gunners equal their biggest Premier League win at Highbury. The Belarusian profits from a collision in the box from Thierry Henry's pass and the ball rolls to him as a result and he makes no mistake from six yards out to make it 7-0 against Middlesbrough.

9 January 2007

Júlio Baptista completes an unforgettable evening for Arsenal and for himself as he becomes the first Gunners player to score four goals at Anfield. The Brazilian arrives in the six-yard box after yet another superb piece of play by Jérémie Aliadière, who chases a long ball down the right flank before skipping past a defender into the box and laying the ball on a plate for Baptista to drill past Jerzy Dudek and put the Gunners into the League Cup semi-final. The goal ends hopes of a dramatic comeback by the hosts who have pulled the score back to 3-5, and the 6-3 win means Liverpool have conceded six goals at Anfield for the first time in 77 years.

4 March 2008

After drawing the Europa League round of 16 first leg against Champions League holders AC Milan 0-0 at the Emirates Stadium, Arsenal look to find the away goal that will mean Milan will have to score twice to win – but they do better than that, grabbing what looks to be a winning goal six minutes from time as Cesc Fàbregas finds the bottom-right corner of the net with a shot from more than 20 yards out.

85

7 April 1973

Taking on Second Division Sunderland in the FA Cup semi-final at Hillsborough, Arsenal can't stop the Wearsiders' epic cup run. Trailing 2-0 to Bob Stokoe's men, the Gunners finally get past the brilliant Sunderland goalkeeper Jim Montgomery as a cross comes in from the left, and after Ray Kennedy swings and misses, Charlie George gets enough contact to see a shot parried by Montgomery – who has made a series of stunning saves throughout the game – but the ball trickles over the line to give the Gunners just a flicker of hope – but it won't be enough and the match finishes 2-1 to Sunderland, who famously go on to beat Leeds United 1-0 in the final.

5 May 1999

Nwankwo Kanu scores a superb individual goal to secure three points and keep Arsenal on track for the Premier League title. Leading 2-1 against Spurs at White Hart Lane and needing victory, the Gunners desperately look for the goal that will seal the win, and when a simple free kick from Patrick Vieira finds sub Kanu on the edge of the box, there seems little on for the skilful Nigerian – but he chests the ball, then flicks it over his shoulder to leave him in on goal and he buries a low shot past Ian Walker to make it 3-1 and keep Arsenal top of the table with just two games remaining.

11 May 2005

Arsenal go 7-0 up to complete a rout over David Moyes's Everton. In what is the biggest win of Arsène Wenger's tenure so far, Thierry Henry torments the Toffees' left-back before sending a cross towards the far post, where José Antonio Reyes touches it back into the path of Mathieu Flamini who makes no mistake from a couple of yards out.

29 October 2011

In a thrilling London derby, Arsenal regain the lead at Stamford Bridge after a calamitous slip from Chelsea captain John Terry. Terry loses his footing and is the last man as Robin van Persie collects the loose ball, runs on and rounds Petr Cech before putting the ball into the empty net and giving the Gunners a 4-3 lead.

29 December 2012

Substitute Olivier Giroud finally gives the Gunners breathing space against Newcastle United. Theo Walcott sends in a fine cross from the right and the French striker arrives on cue to powerfully head home from six yards out and make it 5-3.

86

11 May 1999

A goal that effectively ends Arsenal's 1998/99 Premiership title bid and hands the initiative over to Manchester United. With just two games of the season to go, the Gunners travel to Elland Road to face former Arsenal defender David O'Leary's Leeds United. It has always looked a tough trip in the penultimate fixture, though Arsenal fans are hoping Leeds United's intense rivalry with Manchester United – plus O'Leary's connections to Highbury – will somehow work in their favour. The Gunners go into the game level on points with United and almost identical goal differences, but a host of chances are missed by either side (including a penalty miss by Leeds full-back Ian Harte), which means that when Jimmy Floyd Hasselbaink steals in at the far post to send a diving header past David Seaman, there is not enough time for the Gunners to recover. It leaves Manchester United needing four points from their two remaining games – something Sir Alex Ferguson's side manage with a 0-0 draw against Blackburn and a 2-1 final-day win over (of all clubs) Tottenham Hotspur at Old Trafford. It is a bitter pill for all Arsenal fans to swallow ...

9 December 2000

Thierry Henry receives the ball on the right flank and his first touch takes him clear of the Newcastle United left-back. He gets to the side of the box before looking up and gently lifting a pinpoint cross towards the six-yard box, where Ray Parlour cleverly rises to send an angled header into the bottom-left corner of the net. It's Parlour's second of the afternoon and puts the Gunners 4-0 up at a delighted Highbury.

16 April 2005

Incredibly, the Gunners all but seal a place in their fourth FA Cup Final in five years as Robin van Persie puts Arsène Wenger's side 2-0 up against Blackburn Rovers at the Millennium Stadium in Cardiff. Van Persie cleverly spins away from Rovers centre-half Lucas Neill before advancing into the box and slotting home past Brad Friedel with a low shot into the bottom corner.

87

3 May 1971

Knowing a win or goalless draw will be enough to seal a first top-flight title for 18 years, Arsenal travel to White Hart Lane to take on third-placed Tottenham. Goal average (rather than the goal difference of today) means if the game is tied, only a 0-0 draw will see the Gunners finish above Leeds United. Bertie Mee's side have stuttered in the run-in, drawing 2-2 at West Brom and, crucially, losing 1-0 to Leeds United at Elland Road. But a 1-0 win over Stoke City leaves the Gunners with the scenario they face at White Hart Lane. In a tense, tight affair, John Radford sees his shot superbly saved by Pat Jennings, but George Armstrong is first to the loose ball and his chip back into the middle finds the head of Ray Kennedy, who heads in off the underside of the bar for what will be the winning goal. The title is heading back to Highbury for the first time in 18 years and five days later, the much coveted league and FA Cup double is completed with victory in the FA Cup Final. What a season for Mee's heroic side.

25 November 2003

Already 3-1 up, Arsenal look to punish Serie A giants Inter Milan further in the Champions League group stage clash at the San Siro. Ashley Cole's fine crossfield pass finds Thierry Henry on the right and his low cross is missed by both an Inter defender and the goalkeeper before running free to Edu, who calmly slots an angled shot home to put the Gunners 4-1 up on the night and send the travelling fans into raptures.

8 April 2012

Mikel Arteta scores the only goal of the game to administer what looks like a hammer blow to Manchester City's fading title hopes. The visitors have been reduced to ten men when Mario Balotelli has been dismissed, when the Spaniard wins possession from David Pizarro in midfield before firing a low 25-yard shot past Joe Hart to leave City eight points adrift of leaders Manchester United with six games remaining and seemingly out of contention as a result. It is a deserved win for the Gunners, though City do go on to win the final six games and secure their first title for 44 years, and Arteta will later go on to coach City alongside Pep Guardiola before returning to manage Arsenal in 2019.

29 December 2012

Two goals in two minutes for supersub Olivier Giroud as Newcastle United's defiance wilts in the closing minutes of a thrilling game. Theo Walcott bursts towards the Magpies box before clashing with a defender – a decision could be given either way by the referee who elects to play on – the ball breaks for Giroud, who takes a touch before hitting a low angled shot past the keeper to make it 6-3.

1 November 2016

A goal out of the top drawer and almost a ballet dance of a winner. Mesut Özil breaks the Ludogorets offside trap as he runs on to Mohamed Elneny's excellent through pass, and as the keeper rushes out he calmly lifts the ball over his head and with two defenders racing back, feigns a shot as he cuts inside, putting both of them on their backside, before placing the ball into the net to win the game 3-2 for Arsenal in Bulgaria. Sublime from the German playmaker.

88

26 April 1930

Alex James's superb threaded pass sets Jack Lambert free to drill a low shot past Huddersfield Town's Hugh Turner and put Arsenal 2-0 up. With only seconds remaining after the restart, the Gunners see the game out to win the FA Cup for the first time. The 92,000-plus Wembley crowd has earlier witnessed the ominous site of the low-flying German 776-foot long airship, the *Graf Zeppelin*, casting a huge shadow over the awestruck crowd.

9 January 1979

Having ground out a 1-1 draw in the FA Cup third-round tie away to Sheffield Wednesday, Arsenal are fortunate to stay in the competition against Jack Charlton's Owls, who have gone in at the break leading 1-0. Liam Brady saves the day and earns a second replay with an equaliser two minutes from time, after keeper Chris Turner fails to cut out a cross and the gifted Republic of Ireland playmaker makes no mistake from close range to earn a second replay. At the end of the game, Wednesday boss Charlton refuses to toss a coin for the replay venue and so Leicester City's Filbert Street is chosen.

23 April 1980

Arsenal have been held to a 0-0 draw by Juventus in the European Cup Winners' Cup quarter-final first leg at Highbury. For many, the Italians are strong favourites to progress in the return leg in Turin, but the Gunners remain confident. The second leg proves another tense battle but with two minutes to go, Arsenal secure a dramatic victory as Graham Rix finds 18-year-old Paul Vaessen who makes no mistake to secure a 1-0 win and set up a showdown with Valencia. The victory was also the first home defeat for Juventus by an English side for more than 25 years.

28 October 2000

Arsenal seem to be scoring at will against Manchester City as Thierry Henry wraps up a fine performance with his second in six minutes and the Gunners' fifth of the afternoon. It is Henry who glides through the City midfield before playing the ball to Sylvain Wiltord on the right. The pedestrian City defence are powerless to stop Henry racing past them and on to Wiltord's return pass, where the French striker lifts a shot over Nicky Weaver to make it 5-0 and complete a comprehensive thrashing.

5 December 2001

Breathtaking brilliance from Dennis Bergkamp sets up a third goal for Arsenal against Juventus at Highbury. As the Gunners break forward against the Italian side, Freddie Ljungberg finds Bergkamp just outside the Juve box – the Dutch star holds the ball, moves to his right before twisting back around and then – and only then – is the right time to flick an outrageous pass to Ljungberg, taking out four defenders, and the Swede bundles the ball over Gianluigi Buffon to make it 3-1 and seal victory.

11 May 2003

Freddie Ljungberg completes his hat-trick against Sunderland in the final match of the 2002/03 campaign. With the Stadium of Light by now almost empty of home supporters, the Gunners break one last time with the ball fed to Thierry Henry just outside the Black Cats' box, and he pauses before flicking a short pass to Ljungberg who takes the ball in his stride as he drives towards goal, beats one defender and then slots the ball wide of the keeper. It also completes a hat-trick of assists by Thierry Henry for the Swede.

22 November 2003

Robert Pires applies the *coup de grâce* to victory away to Birmingham City as Arsenal go 3-0 up at St Andrew's. It's typical Arsenal as Thierry Henry toys with two defenders on the left flank before picking out Pires on the edge of the box – he then moves forward, past one defender before rolling the ball past the keeper. It's Henry's third assist of the game and not a bad way to celebrate Arsène Wenger's 400th game in charge, and leaves the Gunners unbeaten in all 15 Premier League games played so far.

11 March 2004

Robert Pires starts and finishes the move that seals a 2-0 win against Blackburn Rovers at Ewood Park. The French winger holds the ball on the left before finding Patrick Vieira on the edge of the box – he finds Gilberto Silva on his right and the Brazilian sees his low shot palmed on to the post by Brad Friedel, but then swept home by Pires following up.

25 April 2006

Jens Lehmann saves one of his best Arsenal displays for when it matters most. Leading Villarreal 1-0 from the first leg of the Champions League semi-final, the La Liga side are gifted a glorious chance to take the tie into extra time when Gaël Clichy is harshly adjudged to have fouled José Mari in the box. The referee points to the penalty spot, but the Gunners' German keeper dives to his left to push away Juan Román Riquelme's spot kick. The final whistle blows not long after and the celebrations begin, with Arsenal booking a place in their first Champions League Final.

24 October 2010

Arsenal complete a comprehensive 3-0 victory over Roberto Mancini's Manchester City with a third goal of the game. City, who have played for most of the game with only ten men, are tormented by Samir Nasri throughout, and it is the French playmaker who releases Nicklas Bendtner to slot home his first of the campaign and seal three points at the Etihad. It's the Gunners' first away clean sheet in 16 games and it helps Arsène Wenger's side leapfrog City into second place in the Premier League. Nasri's starring role actually works against the Gunners with the Blues returning to purchase Nasri 12 months later.

89

14 December 1935

Ted Drake completes a record-breaking day at Villa Park as he bags all seven goals for Arsenal in a 7-1 rout over Aston Villa. Drake has completed a double hat-trick inside the first hour but has to wait until the final minute to claim his seventh, as Cliff Bastin plays the ball into the path of the prolific striker who makes no mistake, creating a new league record in the process. Though Tranmere Rovers' Bunny Bell usurps that feat with nine goals against Oldham Athletic just 12 days later, it is a third-tier fixture and Drake's top-flight record of seven still stands.

11 August 1978

Alan Sunderland pulls a late goal back in the 1979 FA Charity Shield clash with Liverpool at Wembley. Sunderland combines well with Stapleton before finally finding a way past Ray Clemence, but it's too little, too late and is merely a consolation in a 3-1 defeat.

12 May 1979

Alan Sunderland provides the *coup de grâce* to what is regarded as one of the best FA Cup Finals of all time as the Gunners clinch the trophy for a fifth time in the most dramatic finale imaginable. Having led 2-0 until the 86th minute, United stun the Wembley crowd with two goals in two minutes to seemingly send the game to extra time. But Arsenal aren't finished and while

United are still celebrating, Liam Brady drives through the middle before laying a pass off to Graham Rix on the left, and his excellent cross finds Sunderland at the far post to slide home the most dramatic of winning goals and secure a thrilling 3-2 victory for the North London giants.

2 May 1992

Though the race for the Golden Boot seems over, Ian Wright still hasn't given up hope and he scores his second of the afternoon against Southampton in the last minute with a truly memorable individual effort. Wright collects a long throw from David Seaman and races down the left flank, before holding off a challenge from a Saints defender, cutting inside of another defender and drilling a low shot inside the post to make it 4-1 and put him level on goals with Gary Lineker. But it wasn't quite over ...

20 April 1995

Stefan Schwarz grabs a dramatic late goal to save Arsenal's European Cup Winners' Cup hopes away to Sampdoria. Having gone 3-1 behind and with just a couple of minutes remaining, the Gunners are awarded a free kick 30 yards out. Schwarz steps up to fire a low shot that the Sampdoria keeper makes a hash of and only pushes into the bottom corner. With both legs ending 3-2 for the home sides, extra time is needed to decide who goes on into the final.

21 September 1997

A rare but excellent goal for Nigel Winterburn seals three points for Arsenal at Stamford Bridge. Drawing 2-2, Patrick

Vieira plays a short pass to his left where Winterburn is overlapping – the Gunners full-back pushes the ball on and is given plenty of space and time by the Chelsea defenders, so he decides 'why not?' and lets fly with an unstoppable left-foot shot that arrows into the top-right corner from 25 yards out to win the game 3-2.

3 May 1998

Arsenal skipper Tony Adams provides the *coup de grâce* to a title-winning victory with a superb goal virtually on full time. Fittingly, it is Adams's central defensive partner who provides the assist, with Adams breaking out of defence and Bould lifting a clever pass into his path and over the Everton backline, where Adams chests the ball down before thumping a shot past the keeper to complete a 4-0 victory and seal the title with two games to spare. The Gunners are top-flight champions for the 11th time.

25 November 2003

Brilliant work by Jérémie Aliadière sets up Robert Pires to put the icing on the cake of one of Arsenal's greatest European nights. Already leading 4-1 at the San Siro, Aliadière outmuscles the Inter Milan left-back to win the ball and move into the box, where he picks out Pires who rides his luck somewhat as the ball falls kindly for him to slot a low drive into the left of the goal and put the Gunners 5-1 up.

26 December 2003

Thierry Henry completes a comfortable win over Wolves at Highbury. As so often, the goal is a result of Patrick Vieira's ability to intercept and win the ball and after he breaks up another Wolves attack, he plays a short pass to Edu who then plays it to Henry just outside the box. Henry cuts back inside and feigns a shot before cutting back the opposite way, moving past a defender and hitting a low angled shot into the bottom-right corner to make it 3-0. A wonderful finish made to look like simplicity itself.

15 April 2006

Dennis Bergkamp scores his final goal – his 120th for the Gunners – on his final appearance at Highbury. With Arsenal leading 2-1 against West Brom, the brilliant Dutchman, who has come on as a sub and already assisted a goal for Robert Pires, collects the ball some 20 yards out and then curls a shot past the West Brom keeper and into the net to send Highbury – having a 'DB10' day – into raptures. A fitting end to a quite magnificent 11 years with Arsenal.

4 October 2009

Substitute Nicklas Bendtner caps a wonderful team performance with Arsenal's sixth of the afternoon against Blackburn Rovers. The Danish striker has spurned a one-on-one chance moments earlier but he makes no mistake this time, collecting the ball outside the box before cutting in and unleashing a fierce drive that smacks the post and goes in from 18 yards out. It completes a 6-2 rout at the Emirates with Arsène Wenger's men playing some delightful football.

30 October 2012

There is still a glimmer of hope that Arsenal's Capital One Cup adventure is not over when – after being 4-0 down away to Reading – Laurent Koscielny heads home a corner in the last minute of normal time to make it 4-3. It's the second Gunners goal from a corner and it leads to anxious looks from the home supporters as the fourth official prepares to reveal the added time still to be played ...

90

2 May 1992

Determined to win the Golden Boot, Arsenal have one more chance to get Ian Wright the coveted goalscoring award on the final day of the 1991/92 campaign. Alan Smith wins a bouncing ball outside the Southampton box before sending a fine low cross into the six-yard box, where Wright just about manages to bundle the ball over the line via his shin to complete his hat-trick and a 5-1 win for the Gunners. It crowns Wright the season's top scorer and wins him the Golden Boot for the first time. It is also his 31st strike of a memorable campaign and the perfect send-off for the much-loved North Bank terrace which will be bulldozed for an all-seater stand just days later.

23 October 1999

A stunning goal that seals three points at Stamford Bridge and writes Nwankwo Kanu's name into Arsenal folklore. The graceful Nigerian striker wins the ball on the left flank before moving to the far left of the Chelsea box. Keeper Ed de Goey's odd decision to race off his line and challenge Kanu outside the box is a classic rush of blood and the Dutch stopper is easily beaten, leaving Kanu two options – cross into the middle or continue to run in from the left – he chooses neither and instead, from about a yard in from the byline, he curls a shot into the top-right corner of the net, despite the presence of four Chelsea defenders, to not only complete his hat-trick, but complete a third goal in 15 minutes to turn a 2-0 defeat into a 3-2 victory. Brilliant from a very gifted footballer.

22 August 2004

The brilliant Dennis Bergkamp is the architect of yet another wonderful Arsenal goal as he wins possession just inside his own half before carrying the ball into the Middlesbrough half, waiting for the overlapping Robert Pires and then threading a pass into his stride, and his low cross is turned home by Thierry Henry from six yards out to seal a thrilling 5-3 victory. The win means the Gunners have equalled Nottingham Forest's 42-game unbeaten league run, set some 25 years earlier, and extends the length of time since the last Premier League loss to 15 months. An incredible run by an incredible football team.

16 April 2005

Dutch striker Robin van Persie scores his second goal inside four minutes as Arsenal round off an impressive FA Cup semi-final victory over Blackburn Rovers at the Millennium Stadium. Robert Pires, scorer of the Gunners' opening goal in the first half, turns creator with a run down the left flank and cross into the box that van Persie hits first time, and the ball curls just inside the post to put Arsenal 3-0 up in Cardiff.

15 September 2007

One of the best North London derby goals ever? Possibly. Leading 2-1 at White Hart Lane, Arsenal press for a killer third and it arrives in emphatic style through a quite stunning Emmanuel Adebayor volley from the edge of the box. As an attack fizzles out, the ball is played back into the Togo striker's feet – he flicks it up in one move then swivels to hit a thunderbolt of a volley into the top-left corner to secure a 3-1 win. Breathtakingly brilliant.

21 April 2009

Andrey Arshavin looks to have given Arsenal a dramatic last-minute winner at Anfield as he sprints 50 yards to support Theo Walcott who spots his run and plays him through, and Arshavin does the rest, controlling the pass before unleashing a fierce shot past Pepe Reina to make it 4-3 in a Premier League classic – but the scoring isn't over as Liverpool snatch an even later equaliser to claim a 4-4 draw. What a game and what a night for the Gunners' Russian international.

Stoppage time

90+1

21 September 2003

In an explosive end to a game that will be later described as 'The Battle of Old Trafford', Arsenal concede an added-time penalty against Manchester United. The Gunners, already reduced to ten men after Patrick Vieira's sending off, look set to lose their unbeaten start to the campaign as Ruud van Nistelrooy steps up to take the spot kick. The Dutch striker has missed his previous two penalties for United – including one in the Community Shield six weeks earlier – and he sees this one crash against the crossbar as well. The reaction from several Arsenal players towards van Nistelrooy in the fracas that follows leads to fines and criticism from many, but the heat of the moment and the fact the Gunners have made it over the line to claim a 0-0 draw clearly gets the better of one or two individuals in yet another fiery encounter with Sir Alex Ferguson's side, and no love lost between either club at that time ...

7 November 2012

Theo Walcott completes an Emirates rout over Tottenham with the fifth goal of the afternoon. Alex Oxlade-Chamberlain races down the right and into the box before unselfishly squaring to Walcott, who sweeps home a low shot and makes it 5-2 – the same score the Gunners rack up in the previous season's Emirates derby.

90+2

26 May 1989

Drama of the highest calibre at Anfield, but for once, it is in favour of the visitors, not Liverpool. In a thrilling climax to the First Division campaign, Arsenal need to beat the Reds by two clear goals to deny Liverpool an 18th domestic top-flight title. Though 1-0 down, as the game moves into the second minute of added time, it looks as though Liverpool have done enough, but as the ball is played through to Michael Thomas, the Arsenal midfielder sees the ball bounce kindly for him as he tries to control it, and Thomas continues into the box before putting the ball past Bruce Grobbelaar to clinch the title for the Gunners and conclude one of the most dramatic finishes to a top-flight season of all time.

4 March 2008

Arsenal secure a place in the Europa League quarter-finals with a second goal in added time to defeat Champions League holders AC Milan 2-0. Leading through Cesc Fàbregas's 84th-minute strike and with the hosts desperately searching for an equaliser, the Gunners break down the right with Theo Walcott beating Kakha Kaladze before sending a low cross into the six-yard box, where Emmanuel Adebayor makes no mistake with a side-foot finish. It is Milan's first defeat on home soil to an English side but the sporting home fans in the 80,000-plus San Siro crowd applaud Arsenal off the park despite the loss.

29 October 2011

Robin van Persie completes his hat-trick as Arsenal seal three points in a roller-coaster London derby at Stamford Bridge. With Chelsea chasing an added-time equaliser, the Gunners break forward with Mikel Arteta and the Spaniard finds van Persie who immediately hits a venomous left-foot shot that swerves away from Petr Cech and rockets into the roof of the net, completing a memorable 5-3 win.

29 December 2012

Not quite a perfect ten but Arsenal score the tenth goal of an incredible game against Newcastle United – and it is fitting that man of the match Theo Walcott is the scorer, as he completes his hat-trick (to go along with two assists) with a goal that seems impossible. After receiving a short free kick near the left corner flag, Walcott heads in from the left and somehow leaves four defenders in his wake before impudently dinking the ball over the keeper to make it 7-3 – his 14th in all competitions this season.

90+3

9 December 2000

Ray Parlour completes a brilliant hat-trick to wrap up a 5-0 home win over Newcastle United with the last kick of the game. The Gunners knock the ball around deep into injury time when Robert Pires receives the ball just inside the Magpies' half. He weighs up his options and when Ray Parlour sniffs an opportunity, he bursts through the middle, Pires lobs it over the defence and into his path and after controlling the ball on his thigh to move him past the last man he then drills a low shot past Shay Given to complete his hat-trick in style.

27 August 2003

A collective sigh of relief as Arsenal finally put the game against Aston Villa to bed. The visitors have made the Premier League leaders work hard for the narrow 1-0 lead they hold going into added time, but Thierry Henry seals three points as he runs on to Dennis Bergkamp's flick on the left, drifts past the onrushing Villa keeper before slightly adjusting his angle and tucking the ball into the empty net.

28 August 2004

Arsenal complete a 4-1 win over Norwich City with a goal that is made to look so simple. Thierry Henry – involved in all three goals scored before – picks out Dennis Bergkamp's clever run into the box and the Dutchman tees himself up with his first touch and then fires a powerful shot past the keeper with the outside of his right boot to make it 44 Premier League games without losing.

30 May 2015

Arsenal complete perhaps their most comfortable FA Cup triumph yet with a fourth goal against a demoralised and dejected Aston Villa. It is almost too easy as Alex Oxlade-Chamberlain picks the ball up on the right flank, spots Olivier Giroud in the middle and sends a low cross towards the near post, where the unmarked Frenchman nonchalantly flicks the ball home with the outside of his boot to complete a 4-0 rout at Wembley.

26 September 2015

Considering Leicester City will be crowned Premier League champions later in the season, Arsenal's thrashing of the Foxes at the King Power Stadium is all the more impressive. Olivier Giroud puts the icing on the cake in added time as he sweeps home a low Mesut Özil cross from the left to complete a 5-2 victory over Claudio Ranieri's side.

90+4

27 March 1971

Peter Storey dramatically levels for Arsenal against Stoke City in the FA Cup semi-final at Hillsborough. The Gunners have been trailing 2-0 at one stage, but when Stoke's John Mahoney makes a diving save to push Frank McLintock's header away, the referee points to the spot – Gordon Banks is Stoke's keeper! With tremendous pressure on his shoulders, Storey, who has pulled a goal back earlier in the game with a deflected shot, is calmness personified as he coolly rolls a shot inches to the left of a wrong-footed Banks. The goal earns the Gunners a replay and a second crack at getting to their first FA Cup Final in 19 years.

10 February 2004

Thierry Henry finally seals victory against Southampton with his second of the game deep into added time. Robert Pires jinks his way down the right flank before making his way into the box where he plays a low ball towards Gilberto Silva, who mistimes his shot and the ball continues to Henry who shifts inside to lose his marker and then drills home his 101st Gunners goal and makes the score 2-0.

20 October 2015

An excellent interception by Héctor Bellerín sets up the goal that seals victory over Bayern Munich at the Emirates. With Bayern looking to launch one final counter-attack,

Bellerín nips in to win the ball just inside the Bayern half, beats a defender and crosses in to the middle where Mesut Özil sees his shot somehow clawed away by Manuel Neuer – but as the Arsenal players and fans scratch their heads, the referee points to the centre spot with replays and goal-line technology proving the ball has just about crossed the line. The 2-0 win revives hopes the Gunners can progress from Group F despite having lost their opening two group matches.

90+5

14 February 2016

Drama of the highest quality as Arsenal score a late, late winner against Premier League leaders Leicester City. Deep into added time, the Gunners win a free kick on the right flank. Mesut Özil delivers the perfect cross and Danny Welbeck leaps to head the ball into the bottom-left corner of the net and just out of Kasper Schmeichel's reach to send the Emirates wild. It gives the Gunners a 2-1 victory and reduces the gap at the top to just two points. Moreover, it completes the league double over Claudio Ranieri's side who, of course, eventually go on to win the title.

90+6

30 October 2012

Incredible scenes as Arsenal complete a remarkable comeback with almost the last kick of normal time. In time added on to added time, the Gunners again pump a ball into the centre of the Reading back four where Marouane Chamakh stretches every sinew to knock the ball down for Theo Walcott to just get enough power on the ball to get it over the line despite the best efforts of a defender to clear. It makes the score 4-4 and sends this thrilling Capital One Cup tie into extra time, much to the delight of the delirious Gunners fans banked behind the goal.

Extra time

92

21 September 2010

Samir Nasri earns and converts a penalty to put Arsenal 2-1 up in extra time against Spurs. The France international is tugged back in the box by Sebastien Bassong and referee Lee Probert points to the spot. Nasri calmly slots home after sending the keeper the wrong way.

96

21 September 2010

Samir Nasri slots home his second penalty in five minutes to put Arsenal firmly in command in the Carling Cup third-round tie at White Hart Lane. Already 2-1 up, referee Lee Probert awards another spot kick to the Gunners after Stephen Caulker grabs the arm of sub Marouane Chamakh inside the box, and Nasri again sends the Spurs keeper the wrong way to make it 3-1 in extra time.

99

18 November 1997

Dennis Bergkamp scores what will prove to be the only goal of an attritional League Cup third round tie with Coventry City at Highbury. After the Sky Blues have held out for 0-0 in normal time, Bergkamp breaks the deadlock to the relief of most of the 30,199 home crowd.

100

14 January 1998

Arsenal finally edge ahead in the FA Cup third-round clash with Port Vale. After being held to a 0-0 draw at Highbury by the First Division side, the replay at Vale Park also ends goalless and extra time ensues. The Gunners, looking for one piece of magic to break a defence that has held out for exactly 200 minutes, find it when Dennis Bergkamp curls a superb shot into the top-right corner of the Vale net. Vale level on 112 minutes to take the tie to penalties and Arsenal breathe a huge sigh of relief when they triumph 4-3 on spot kicks.

101

8 May 1971

Arsenal, looking to win the FA Cup for the first time in 21 years, are up against the side they played and beat back in 1950 – Liverpool – but after both sides fail to score in normal time, the match goes into extra time. Within two minutes, Steve Heighway has put the Reds ahead, but the Gunners level nine minutes later with a scrambled goal from close range that George Graham initially claims – but TV replays prove it is Eddie Kelly who has got the final touch and thus becomes the first substitute to ever score in the FA Cup Final.

23 April 2017

Having come back from a goal behind in normal time and then see Manchester City hit the woodwork twice in the time that remains, the Gunners ride their luck somewhat in the 2017 FA Cup semi-final at Wembley. But in the first half of extra time, Alexis Sánchez finally gives Arsenal the lead – and it is enough to book yet another FA Cup Final appearance for the club that has dominated the competition over the years. As a free kick from the right comes in, City fail to clear and the ball falls to Sánchez, who takes a slight touch before tucking the ball into the bottom-left corner from a couple of yards out to seal a 2-1 win.

103

30 October 2012

Arsenal finally have the lead in the Capital One Cup fourth-round tie away to Reading. Despite trailing 4-0 in the first half, the comeback seems complete when – after some nice interplay on the left – the ball finds its way to Marouane Chamakh, who drills a low shot into the bottom-left corner from 18 yards out to send the travelling Arsenal supporters wild with delight.

105

21 September 2010

Andrey Arshavin scores Arsenal's third goal in the first half of extra time at White Hart Lane to make it 4-1 and seal the Carling Cup third-round tie. Arshavin reacts first to a quickly taken free kick to fire home from close range and send thousands of Tottenham fans heading for the exits and the Gunners into the next round.

108

24 January 2006

Robin van Persie scores a superb free kick to put Arsenal within sight of the League Cup Final. The Gunners have levelled the semi-final second leg aggregate thanks to Thierry Henry's 65th-minute goal when a free kick is awarded slightly to the right of the Wigan Athletic box and 25 yards or so out. van Persie takes his time, lines up his sights and curls a left-foot shot into the top-right corner of the Wigan net to make it 2-1 in extra time. There will be a sting in the tail, however, as Jason Roberts scores in the 119th minute to send Wigan through on away goals.

14 February 2007

Sub Jérémie Aliadière makes a superb run and pass to Freddie Ljungberg as Arsenal go 2-1 up away to Bolton Wanderers in the FA Cup fifth-round replay tie at the Reebok Stadium. The game has ended 1-1 in normal time with the hosts scoring a last-gasp leveller – but the Gunners resume control as Ljungberg tucks a low shot into the bottom-right corner from 18 yards.

109

17 May 2014

Having trailed 2-0 after just eight minutes of the 2014 FA Cup Final against Hull City, Arsenal complete their comeback with what proves to be an extra-time winning goal. With the Gunners in the ascendency, Olivier Giroud races into the Hull penalty area before laying a back-flick into the path of Aaron Ramsey, and the Arsenal midfielder makes no mistake from 12 yards with a crisp low drive to make it 3-2 and secure victory – the club's 11th success in the competition.

111

8 May 1971

Arsenal complete an extra-time comeback as Charlie George scores a superb goal to give the Gunners a 2-1 FA Cup Final win over Liverpool. Having levelled in the first half of extra time through Eddie Kelly's scuffed effort, Arsenal have more energy and drive than Liverpool in the closing stages, and when John Radford plays the ball inside to George, he thumps a rising shot past Ray Clemence from the edge of the box to score what proves to be the winning goal. George then lays down on the Wembley turf for one of the most memorable celebrations the old stadium has ever seen and the Gunners go on to see out the time that remains and claim a fourth FA Cup success.

120

14 February 2007

With Bolton Wanderers – by now reduced to ten men – chasing an unlikely extra-time equaliser at the Reebok, Arsenal break down the field to finally end Sam Allardyce's side's resistance and book an FA Cup quarter-final berth with Blackburn Rovers. Júlio Baptista has virtually the whole of the Bolton half to himself as he breaks clear with Emmanuel Adebayor alongside him. As the Brazilian takes the ball around the keeper, Adebayor almost nicks it off his toes to roll it into the empty net and secure a 3-1 victory.

Extra-time stoppage time

120+1

20 May 1993

Arsenal win the FA Cup for the sixth time and the second time victory has been achieved in extra time. The Gunners and Sheffield Wednesday can't be separated in normal time of the FA Cup Final replay at Wembley, but with almost the last action of the game, Arsenal score a dramatic winner. In additional time at the end of extra time, Paul Merson's corner finds the head of Andy Linighan and Owls goalkeeper Chris Woods makes a hash of his attempted save and fumbles the ball over the line to send the Gunners fans wild and secure a 2-1 victory.

21 December 2005

Arsenal come mightily close to a huge League Cup upset away to third-tier Doncaster Rovers. The Gunners have fallen behind after just two minutes at the Keepmoat Stadium but fight back to level after the break. The game moves into extra time and the hosts again go in front, with a place in the semi-finals at stake – and when the board for added time in extra time goes up, Arsenal look certain to exit the competition. Then, a final break forward with Emmanuel Eboué racing down the right flank – Gilberto Silva makes a superb burst alongside him into the box and when the cross finds the Brazilian he slides home the equaliser to make it 2-2 and force penalties.

The Gunners triumph 3-1 on spot kicks to leave the home fans scratching their heads at how Arsenal have snatched victory from the jaws of defeat.

30 October 2012

In added time in extra time of a quite incredible Capital One Cup fourth-round tie, Arsenal regain the lead against Reading at the Madejski Stadium. The Royals have made it 5-5 just minutes earlier and the crowd are preparing for a penalty shoot-out when Andrey Arshavin's jinking run ends with a low shot that is partially cleared off the line, only for Theo Walcott to slam home from close range to complete his hat-trick and make it 6-5 to the Gunners.

120+3

30 October 2012

Game, set and match – finally! Arsenal go 7-5 up and seal victory in one of the most amazing Capital One Cup ties of all time, as Reading's Gunter misses a header and allows Marouane Chamakh to race clear and then lob Adam Federici from 25 yards out to end a thrilling contest at the Madejski Stadium and write a new chapter under '12-goal thrillers' into club folklore.

Penalty shoot-outs

14 May 1980

Arsenal and Valencia cannot be separated in the 1980 European Cup Winners' Cup Final at the Heysel Stadium in Belgium. After 90 minutes, the score is 0-0 and a further 30 minutes fails to produce a goal between two evenly matched sides. A penalty shoot-out – the Gunners' first official penalty shoot-out – ensues ...

- Mario Kempes (Valencia) – saved by Pat Jennings – 0-0
- Liam Brady (Arsenal) – saved by Carlos Pereira – 0-0
- Daniel Solsona (Valencia) – scores – 1-0
- Frank Stapleton (Arsenal) – scores – 1-1
- Pablo Rodríguez (Valencia) – scores – 2-1
- Alan Sunderland (Arsenal) – scores – 2-2
- Ángel Castellanos (Valencia) – scores – 3-2
- Brian Talbot (Arsenal) – scores – 3-3
- Rainer Bonhof (Valencia) – scores – 4-3
- John Hollins (Arsenal) – scores – 4-4
- Ricardo Arias (Valencia) – scores – 5-4
- Graham Rix (Arsenal) – saved by Carlos Pereira – 5-4

Valencia win 5-4 on penalties.

20 April 1995

After the European Cup Winners' Cup semi-final second leg ends with Arsenal and Sampdoria locked at 5-5 on aggregate, a penalty shoot-out ensues to decide the winner ...

- Lee Dixon (Arsenal) – scores – 0-1
- Siniša Mihajlović (Sampdoria) – saved by David Seaman – 0-1
- Eddie McGoldrick (Arsenal) – fires over the crossbar – 0-1
- Vladimir Jugović (Sampdoria) – saved by David Seaman – 0-1
- John Hartson (Arsenal) – scores – 0-2
- Riccardo Maspero (Sampdoria) – scores – 1-2
- Tony Adams (Arsenal) – scores – 1-3
- Moreno Mannini (Sampdoria) – scores – 2-3
- Paul Merson (Arsenal) – saved by Walter Zenga – 2-3
- Attilio Lombardo (Sampdoria) – saved by David Seaman – 2-3

Arsenal win 3-2 on penalties.

28 October 2003

Arsenal survive a mighty scare at Highbury against Rotherham United of the third tier. Despite taking the lead through Jérémie Aliadière on 11 minutes, Darren Byfield equalises in the 90th minute for the visitors and after a further 30 minutes of extra time can't separate the teams, the game goes to penalties. Cesc Fàbregas makes his debut in this game and becomes the youngest player ever to represent the Gunners, aged 16 years and 177 days old.

- Sylvain Wiltord (Arsenal) – misses – 0-0
- Chris Swailes (Rotherham United) – scores – 0-1

- Edu Gaspar (Arsenal) – scores – 1-1
- Martin McIntosh (Rotherham United) – scores – 1-2
- Jérémie Aliadière (Arsenal) – scores – 2-2
- John Mullin (Rotherham United) – misses – 2-2
- Pascal Cygan (Arsenal) – scores – 3-2
- Julien Baudet (Rotherham United) – scores – 3-3
- Quincy Owusu-Abeyie (Arsenal) – misses – 3-3
- Darren Byfield (Rotherham United) – misses – 3-3
- Nwankwo Kanu (Arsenal) – scores – 4-3
- Paul Hurst (Rotherham United) – scores – 4-4
- John Spicer (Arsenal) – scores – 5-4
- Paul Warne (Rotherham United) – scores – 5-5
- Ryan Smith (Arsenal) – scores – 6-5
- Shaun Barker (Rotherham United) – scores – 6-6
- Gaël Clichy (Arsenal) – scores – 7-6
- Richie Barker (Rotherham United) – scores – 7-7
- Graham Stack (Arsenal) – scores – 8-7
- Gary Montgomery (Rotherham United) – scores – 8-8
- Sylvain Wiltord (Arsenal) – scores – 9-8
- Chris Swailes (Rotherham United) – misses – 9-8

Arsenal win 9-8 on penalties.

21 May 2005

Normal time and extra time can't separate fierce Premier League rivals Arsenal and Manchester United in the 2005 FA Cup Final at the Millennium Stadium in Cardiff. Though there are chances for both teams, the match ends 0-0 and goes to a penalty shoot-out. It is the Gunners who hold their nerve, converting all five spot kicks to win the trophy 5-4 – a tenth FA Cup triumph for the Gunners, who have made the competition their own. It is also the first time in FA Cup history that the final is settled by a penalty shoot-out.

- Ruud van Nistelrooy (Manchester United) – scores – 0-1
- Lauren (Arsenal) – scores – 1-1
- Paul Scholes (Manchester United) – saved by Jens Lehmann – 1-1
- Freddie Ljungberg (Arsenal) – scores – 2-1
- Cristiano Ronaldo (Manchester United) – scores – 2-2
- Robin van Persie (Arsenal) – scores – 3-2
- Wayne Rooney (Manchester United) – scores – 3-3
- Ashley Cole (Arsenal) – scores – 4-3
- Roy Keane (Manchester United) – scores – 4-4
- Patrick Vieira (Arsenal) – scores – 5-4

Arsenal win 5-4 on penalties.

11 March 2009

Arsenal lose a tense Champions League second leg with AS Roma and the 1-0 scoreline in favour of the Italians means the aggregate is level at 1-1 and a penalty shoot-out is needed to settle the tie with a place in the quarter-finals at stake.

- Eduardo (Arsenal) – saved by Doni – 0-0
- David Pizarro (Roma) – scores – 1-0
- Robin van Persie (Arsenal) – scores – 1-1
- Mirko Vučinić (AS Roma) – saved by Manuel Almunia – 1-1
- Theo Walcott (Arsenal) – scores – 1-2
- Júlio Baptista (AS Roma) – scores – 2-2
- Samir Nasri (Arsenal) – scores – 2-3
- Vincenzo Montella (AS Roma) – scores – 3-3
- Denílson (Arsenal) – scores – 3-4
- Francesco Totti (AS Roma) – scores – 4-4
- Kolo Touré (Arsenal) – scores – 4-5
- Alberto Aquilani (AS Roma) – scores – 5-5
- Bacary Sagna (Arsenal) – scores – 5-6

- John Arne Riise (AS Roma) – scores – 6-6
- Abou Diaby (Arsenal) – scores – 6-7
- Max Tonetto (AS Roma) – misses – 6-7

Arsenal win 7-6 on penalties.

12 April 2014

Arsenal are held to a 1-1 draw by Championship side and FA Cup holders Wigan Athletic. The teams end 90 minutes at 1-1 and can't be separated in extra time, leading to the Gunners' second penalty shoot-out at Wembley. With a place in the final awaiting the winners, it is the Gunners who hold their nerve to win the penalty shoot-out 4-2.

- Stephen Caldwell (Wigan Athletic) – saved by Łucasz Fabiański – 0-0
- Mikel Arteta (Arsenal) – scores – 0-1
- Jack Collison (Wigan Athletic) – saved by Łucasz Fabiański – 0-1
- Kim Källström (Arsenal) – scores – 0-2
- Jean Beausejour (Wigan Athletic) – scores – 1-2
- Olivier Giroud (Arsenal) – scores – 1-3
- James McArthur (Wigan Athletic) – scores – 2-3
- Santi Cazorla (Arsenal) – scores – 2-4

Arsenal win 4-2 on penalties.

6 August 2017

After Arsenal draw 1-1 with Chelsea in the FA Community Shield clash at Wembley, the game goes straight to penalties in order to decide the winners. Using the new A-B-B-A-A-B-B-A-B method the shoot-out ensues ...

- Gary Cahill (Chelsea) – scores – 0-1
- Theo Walcott (Arsenal) – scores – 1-1

- Nacho Monreal (Arsenal) – scores – 2-1
- Thibaut Courtois (Chelsea) – shoots over the crossbar – 2-1
- Alvaro Morata (Chelsea) – misses – 2-1
- Alex Oxlade-Chamberlain (Arsenal) – scores – 3-1
- Olivier Giroud (Arsenal) – scores – 4-1

Arsenal win 4-1 on penalties.

30 October 2019

Arsenal twice throw a two-goal lead away during an incredible 5-5 Carabao Cup fourth-round tie at Anfield. The match goes straight to penalties ...

- Héctor Bellerín (Arsenal) – scores – 0-1
- James Milner (Liverpool) – scores – 1-1
- Matteo Guendouzi (Arsenal) – scores – 1-2
- Adam Lallana (Liverpool) – scores – 2-2
- Gabriel Martinelli (Arsenal) – scores – 2-3
- Rhian Brewster (Liverpool) – scores – 3-3
- Dani Ceballos (Arsenal) – saved by Caoimhin Kelleher – 3-3
- Divock Origi (Liverpool) – scores – 4-3
- Ainsley Maitland-Niles (Arsenal) – scores – 4-4
- Curtis Jones (Liverpool) – scores – 5-4

Liverpool win 5-4 on penalties.

394 goals